LOK VIRSA

❈ CULTURAL VOYAGE ❈

Exploring the Muslim Heritage

To MR. Tinniswood.

I Wish You a Merry Christmas and
A Happy New Year.

16/12/08

Makhdoom Chishti

Dedicated to the late Tahir Hussain Chishti
His motto was *"live for others"*.

LOK VIRSA

CULTURAL VOYAGE

Exploring the Muslim Heritage

Compiled by Makhdoom Ahmad Chishti

Editorial panel:

Mr Makhdoom Ahmad Chishti, SUFI Trust Ltd
Miss Verdah Chishti, Birmingham City Council
Dr. Malcolm Dick, University of Birmingham
Mrs Alison Gove-Humphries, Birmingham City Council
Miss Aasma Nazir, Birmingham City Council

BREWIN BOOKS

First published by
Brewin Books Ltd, 56 Alcester Road,
Studley, Warwickshire B80 7LG in 2008
on behalf of
The Social Unity Foundation of Innovation (SUFI) Trust Ltd.
Registered office: 7 Rolling Mill Close, Edgbaston, Birmingham, B5 7QD.

www.brewinbooks.com

ISBN: 978-1-85858-308-2

A Cataloguing in Publication Record
for this title is available from the British Library.

Design by Brewin Books. Typeset in Galliard.
Made & Printed in Great Britain
by Warwick Printing Ltd.

Bismillah hir Rahman nir Raheem

"In the name of Allah, most Gracious, most Compassionate"

Whoever travels without a guide needs
two hundred years for a two day journey

(Jalāluddin Rūmī, Mathnawi)

Contents

Acknowledgements

This book is the result of the collaborative, imaginative and collective efforts of many individuals who supported the work of the Lok Virsa (Cultural Voyage) Project. The work would not have been possible without the financial support provided by the Heritage Lottery Fund.

A number of scholars and people from local communities, both Muslim and non-Muslim, contributed to the final manuscript. In particular, I am grateful to those who worked alongside me in the Lok Virsa Project, Dr Malcolm Dick of the University of Birmingham, Verdah Chishti, Alison Gove-Humphries and Aasma Nazir, all of Birmingham City Council, who have contributed articles, commissioned pieces from others, secured individual stories and helped to shape and edit the manuscript.

Some of the personal stories come from oral histories conducted by the Millennibrum Project in 2000 and 2001. This was a multi-media community history project, which created a large archive of post-1945 resources for Birmingham City Archives, Birmingham Central Library and Birmingham Museums & Art Gallery. This project was financed by the Millennium Commission and managed for the Birmingham City Council by the University of Central England.

At different stages during the life of Lok Virsa, several people provided support, encouragement and advice. They were Lin Homer, formerly Chief Executive, Birmingham City Council, Rita McLean, Acting Director, Birmingham Museums & Art Gallery and Sian Roberts, Birmingham City Archives in Birmingham Central Library, Director of the Connecting Histories Project, another community-based project funded by the Heritage Lottery Fund. Members of Birmingham Central Mosque and the Equality and Diversity Division supplied a great deal of assistance. The Trustees of the SUFI Trust contributed significantly to Lok Virsa, as did several volunteers at different stages in the life of the project. My wife, Tahseen Akhtar Chishti, and family also gave their active support to the work of Lok Virsa.

Other individuals provided professional assistance at various times. Gareth Lewis photographed a number of places, people and things to produce a range of unique images. Brigitte Winsor, Birmingham City Archives, scanned various illustrations and photographs which were used to support the text of this publication. Muhammad Azeem, Nasir Farooqi, Muhammad Ali and Muhammad Talha Bukhari provided translation of Arabic scripts and Islamic art calligraphy.

Bollywood Wholesale Distributors, Al-Yafai for Orientals and the Orinetal Rug Centre kindly allowed the project to photograph the musical instruments, artefacts and rugs, they had for sale. Lahore Sweet and Kebab House allowed the photography of food preparation on their premises in Ladypool Road. Judith Watkin proofread the final manuscript and Realla Kauser prepared captions for the illustrations. Finally, my thanks go to the team at Brewin Books for producing a first-rate publication.

Makhdoom Ahmad Chishti

Director, SUFI Trust and Lok Virsa

Time

Recognise the importance of time
For time stands for no man
Nor does it obey any command
Try and understand what time has to say
For one who loses time cannot find it again
Realise the priceless value of time
For once time has gone forward it does not move backward
So learn your lesson and respect time

Wahid Azeez, Year 9, The Woodrush High School, Worcestershire.

Introduction

Lok Virsa (cultural voyage) is a project to create an awareness of the experiences and legacies of diverse Muslim communities living in Birmingham. The idea for compiling this book arose from a vision to find common threads in our lives to enable us to understand each other's behaviour. This vision is particularly important in the twenty-first century when international conflict, terrorism, the 'War on Terror' and religious and racial tension mark the contemporary world.

The project developed from the work of Social Unity Foundation of Innovation (SUFI) Trust. This is a charitable trust that has several aims:

❶ To develop a programme which will contribute towards the formation of networks and partnerships, support integration, provide opportunities to develop projects, access information, enable self-development and create discussion groups to encourage individuals to get involved in issues of relevance to communities living and working in a global society.

❷ To associate the wider community, the statutory and non-statutory organisations, voluntary groups and individuals in a common effort to advance education and social welfare with the object of improving conditions of life for the community.

❸ To encourage all sectors of the Black and ethnic communities to participate in celebrating their own achievements.

❹ To disseminate information about the variety of achievements in education, employment, sport and arts, the local community and other fields of influence.

❺ To develop links with schools, youth groups, and other community organisations in all matters relating to the promotion of cross-cultural working and pride.

❻ To raise funds for future objectives of the organisation's programmes.

This publication provides information and stories to enhance understanding of the present circumstances of Muslim communities in Birmingham and their historical evolution. It looks at the relationships between culture and religion and aims to provide an insight into the experiences of individuals who are practising Muslims or who come from communities with a predominantly Muslim background originating in South and Central Asia, the Middle East, Africa and Europe.

Islam is a major world religion. It is estimated that the number of Muslims worldwide ranges from 750 milion to 1.2 billion. There are around 1.6 million Muslims in Britain.

According to the 2001 census, there were over 140,000 people who defined themselves as Muslims in Birmingham in a city of slightly less than one million people. These communities contain many children and young people, so their numbers and impact are likely to increase as time progresses. This book provides a record of these communities at a time when they are playing an important part in local and national life.

The five sections in the book look at aspects of the Muslim experience. The first section, *Muslim Communities*, looks at the historical, international and contemporary dimensions of groups, individuals and organisations which comprise a large and diverse population. Chapters explore local experiences and institutions and present autobiographies and biographies provided by Birmingham people. The second section, *Celebrations and Cultures*, illustrates aspects of public and daily life. The third section, *Windows on Islam* presents the core teachings of Islam, an understanding of the Islamic Year and religious festivals and perspectives on Muslim life and relationships. One of the features of this section is a focus on individual beliefs through the words and images of local Muslims. The fourth section, *Art and Artefacts* portrays the creative activity of Muslim craftwork and artists. The fifth section, *Cultural Enrichment* combines chapters on Sufism, music of various kinds, dancing, rugs, sport and architecture with information about the resources available to represent and investigate the Muslim Heritage. Throughout, images and photographs illustrate the words in the text. The publication also provides a glossary of technical terms and words from Arabic and other Asian languages which are used in the book.

Many cultural traditions are in danger of becoming history. This book presents the beliefs, lives, traditions and cultures of Muslim communities as experiences in which we can all share.

Makhdoom Ahmad Chishti

⊙ *Turkish art of illuminated paintings [Courtesy of COL Cards].*

Section A
Muslim Communities

Muslim Communities: Introduction

This section provides an insight into the history and contemporary circumstances of different communities in Birmingham and the West Midlands which have originated in countries overseas with a substantial Muslim religious background. The pieces are written by several individuals, both Muslim and non-Muslim. They provide general surveys, statistical information, overviews of different communities, studies of organisations and individual biographies or autobiographies which present varied perspectives and experiences. The West Midlands has been home to men and women from Muslim communities who have contributed to local life as community activists, religious leaders, politicians, academics, lawyers, artists, engineers and workers of many different kinds. One theme that emerges is the importance of networks through families, communities and institutions, in maintaining identity and providing support. The articles and stories which follow cannot do justice to every group or individual. Instead they pinpoint some of the diverse traditions, cultures, expectations and experiences which have contributed to Birmingham's evolution as a multi-cultural city.

Malcolm Dick

The Origins of local Muslim Communities

Cultural and religious diversity has been an integral part of Birmingham's history for hundreds of years. The contemporary situation for Muslims is part of a lengthy experience of migration of new communities into Birmingham. The Welsh were probably the first ethnic minority to settle in Birmingham. They were conquered by the English in medieval times and spoke a different language. As drovers of cattle from the Welsh countryside and traders they contributed to the local economy. Streets such as

⬆ *Alum Rock, Saltley, Birmingham.*

⬅ *The busy streets of Alum Rock are home to a body of multicultural communities. Alum Rock's restaurants attract local people as well as tourists who choose to acquire a taste for Eastern cuisine. The merchandise traded in its extensive shops reflect its rich diversity.*

Welch End and the Welch Cross were former testimonies of Birmingham's Welsh connection. We know little about the lives of Welsh people in Birmingham before the eighteenth century, but their experiences must have been similar to those of other minorities who came to Birmingham in more recent times. In the eighteenth and nineteenth centuries, Catholic and Protestant Irish people escaped poverty to find work, and Jewish settlers fled persecution in Central and Eastern Europe to settle in the town. These minorities lived initially in the poorest districts of Birmingham where the men worked mostly, but not exclusively, in unskilled or casual occupations. We also know from the baptism and burial records of local churches that Birmingham was home to a small number of Black people from Africa, the Caribbean and the USA in the eighteenth and nineteenth centuries.

We have tantalising glimpses of connections between Birmingham, the West Midlands and the Muslim world before the twentieth century. The first possible reference is in the Churchwardens' accounts of the Parish of Northfield in 1684 which refers to the sum of 6d 'Given to 9 soldiers from Tangeare' or Tangiers in Morocco, North Africa. Under Poor Law regulations, local churchwardens in each Church of England parish had to billet soldiers travelling with passes through their locality. If these were Muslim soldiers on a journey through this part of the Midlands, there is no explanation of why they were in the area.

By the early nineteenth century, the Muslim world was linked economically to the West Midlands. Examples from company records show that regional firms were trading with parts of the world inhabited by Muslims. In the 1820s the firm of Boulton and Watt was supplying steam engines to power the mints which produced coins for the East India Company at Calcutta and Bombay in British India. In 1823 the Shah of Persia ordered porcelain from the Worcester factory of Messrs Flight and Co. In 1865, Nawob Nazin of Bengal visited the

settled Muslim community in Birmingham was composed of men from the Yemen in the late 1930s. They established the first mosque in the city in the 1940s. Since then Muslims have come to Birmingham from Asia, Africa and Eastern Europe. Other individuals from Britain and the Caribbean have converted to the faith. The Census in 2001 provided a record of the religious affiliation of local residents. Out of a total population of 977,099, 140,033 individuals described themselves as Muslims, roughly 14% of the population and the largest proportion of any town in the West Midlands.

Malcolm Dick

○ *Ladypool Road, Balsall Heath, Birmingham.*

Soho Foundry in Handsworth. His visit was one of several to local factories by princes and nobility from British India in the nineteenth century.

There were a small number of Muslim residents in the West Midlands at this time. A letter from the firm of Boulton & Watt to Naysmyth & Co in 1843 refers to a man called Affifi Salah who lived in Redditch and was working for Samuel Thomas, a local needle manufacturer in the town. Shropshire was also home to Asam Ali who was born in the 'City of Mecca, Saudi Arabia'. At the time of the 1861 Census he was a 44 year-old vendor of tracts and stayed with his Irish-born wife in a lodging house in Shrewsbury. Ten years later he was living in Ludlow. In 1869 a Christian missionary, Joseph Salter described a visit to a lodging house for Asians in Birmingham, one of three for Asians in the town. It is likely that a number of these men were Muslims. Research into census returns and other local archives may well tell us more about Muslims who lived in the West Midlands in the nineteenth and early twentieth centuries.

In the mid-twentieth century, the Muslim presence in Birmingham became an important one. The first permanent,

References

1. Dick, Malcolm, *Birmingham: a History of the City and its People* (Birmingham City Council, 2005).
2. Dick, Malcolm, *Celebrating Sanctuary, Birmingham and the Refugee Experience 1750 – 2002* (Birmingham, Refugee Action, 2002).
3. Grosvenor, Ian, McLean, Rita and Roberts, Sîan (eds), *Making Connections, Birmingham Black International History* (Birmingham City Council, 2002).
4. Joly, Daniele, *Britannia's Crescent: making a Place for Muslims in British Society* (Aldershot, 1995).
5. Tait, Fiona, *Black History Sources in Birmingham City Archives* (Birmingham City Council, 2004).
6. Trinder, Barrie, *The Market Town Lodging House in Victorian England*, (Leicester, Friends of the Centre for English Local History, 2001).

3

The Development of local Muslim Communities

Muslims in Britain

Since the nineteenth century there has been a Muslim presence in Britain. Muslims from the Raj came to Britain to study or engage in commerce and seamen and traders began settling around the major British ports. The growth of the Muslim population, however, dates from the post-war immigration of Pakistanis, Bangladeshis and Indians, who arrived to fill specific labour shortages in largely declining industrial sectors. During the 1990s, there was an intake of European and Middle Eastern Muslim 'refugees and asylum seekers' from such places as Bosnia, Kosovo, Afghanistan, Somalia, and Iraq, but the demographic profile today is dominated by Muslims from South Asia, and, principally, from Pakistan and Bangladesh (approximately half of all Muslims in Britain are 'Pakistani').

The independence of former East Pakistan in the early 1970s and the fact that the vast majority of Pakistanis in Britain are from the Azad (Free) Kashmir region does, however, mask the true ethnic identities of people ordinarily identified as Pakistanis. Furthermore, there is a considerable body of people who originate from the North West frontier. Because of huge population movements from Afghanistan to Pakistan because of the Russian-Afghan War, political instability following the war, the Taliban era and the United Nations invasion of Afghanistan in the twenty-first century, ethnic identities such as Pukhtun or Pathan are subsumed under that of Pakistani. In general, post-war South Asian Muslims largely entered and settled in Britain as a workforce for the jobs indigenous people did not wish to carry out

anymore. Today, the various South Asian Muslim groups continue to live excluded lives, existing at the bottom of local economies and societies in post-industrial cities in the North, the Midlands, and the South that are in the process of redeveloping an economic and social base. Muslims are often excluded from this experience because of structural subordination and existing conditions of poverty, disadvantage, and alienation.

According to the 2001 Census, around 1m of Britain's 1.6m Muslims originate from South Asia (0.75m are from Pakistan and the remainder from Bangladesh and India). Other Muslims are from North Africa, Eastern Europe, and South East Asia. One third of all British Muslims are under the age of 14. There are 7.2m people in London, and 1m are Muslims. In a city of 1m Brummies, Muslims account for 14.3 per cent of the population, with Pakistanis numbering just over 104,000. This number is twice as large as the highest concentration of Muslims outside of London. In 2001, nearly one in ten of all British Muslims were to be found in Birmingham, arguably home to the world's largest expatriate Kashmiri community.

On the whole, British South Asian Muslims remain concentrated in the inner city areas of older towns and cities in the North, the Midlands and the South. The British Muslim population has grown from 21,000 in 1951 to 1.6m today.

Muslims in Birmingham

Birmingham is Britain's 'second city'. Until the 1960s, the West Midlands region, with Birmingham at its centre, was one of the fastest growing. Vehicles, metal manufacturing and engineering provided the strength of the industrial base. During the 1970s and 1980s, however, the region suffered severe industrial decline with the city of Birmingham particularly affected. Unemployment rose far faster than new jobs were being created with some wards in the inner cities decimated as a result. As the indigenous population moved out of inner Birmingham, through a process known

⬆ *Edward Road, Balsall Heath, Birmingham. Edward Road is an area known for immigrants. It was once the residence of Jewish settlers and is currently home to the Yemeni community. Its historic links with all foreign countries shows an excellent example of interdependent communities living reciprocally. It is also where Birmingham's very first mosque was established.*

as 'white flight', South Asian Muslims were trapped in the inner city areas. Subsequently, these areas became further impoverished with new employment being created elsewhere and in other economic sectors. It is only recently that the expanding service sector has begun to make an impact on the fortunes of city. The effects of de-industrialisation, technological investment, and the internationalisation of capital and labour have left a distinct impression on some parts of the city.

Today, there are noticeable ethnic and religious communities, past and present, living in reasonable harmony. This is irrespective of how successfully or otherwise the local state has managed its multicultural and public policy relations. More recently, Birmingham is becoming home to Africans gravitating to the city and moving (or being moved) to already densely populated South Asian Muslim areas. These new Muslim groups arrive to live and work in the city and want to be near existing established Muslim and other ethnic minority communities in a city where one-in-three are non-white. As 'refugees and asylum seekers', new Muslim immigrant groups can often find it harder to integrate into society. Much of this is a function of limited economic,

cultural and social capital as well as the facts of racism and discrimination. New and existing Muslim groups encounter issues in accessing employment, housing, and education, while at the same time they are vulnerable to hostility from the dominant society where public opinion, whipped up by media sensationalism and right-wing nationalism, is especially unsympathetic.

Government policy in this area tends to be one of 'integration with cultural tolerance' but the striking feature of the structural experience of British Muslims, new and old, is the economic and social positions they possess. Birmingham South Asian Muslims experience some of the highest rates of unemployment, with up to three times the overall city levels. These inner city areas show that it is Muslims (largely Pakistanis and Bangladeshis but also Somalis and Yemenis) who occupy them in highest numbers and that it is they who are at greatest disadvantage (for example, in the wards of Aston, Ladywood, Moseley, Small Heath, Saltley, Sparkhill, Sparkbrook, and Washwood Heath). In Birmingham, most South Asian Muslims appear to have been particularly neglected by state and third way public services. This group constitutes one of the most marginalised, alienated, isolated, discriminated against, and misunderstood groups in society. It is difficult to generate a position of cultural and social integration from a weak economic and social base.

Tahir Abbas

References

1. Abbas, T, *The Education of British South Asians* (Basingstoke: Palgrave-Macmillan, 2004).
2. Abbas, T, (ed), *Muslim Britain: Communities under Pressure* (Zed, 2005).
3. Abbas, T. and M. Anwar, "An Analysis of Race Equality Policy and Practice in the City of Birmingham, UK", *Local Government Studies*, 31(1): 53–68.

Muslim Communities: a statistical portrait

Faith

The worldwide Muslim community, which is known in Arabic as the *'Ummah'*, contains about one billion adherents. The Muslim community in the UK is probably over 1.6 million. Included in the 2001 Census was a question asking people to indicate their faith. This was a voluntary tick box exercise, from which it was possible to estimate the size of different faith communities in the UK in a total population of 59 million. From this 92% answered this question. It is therefore possible that the number of Muslims in the table is under-represented.

Faiths	Number of People	Percentage
Christians	42m	71
Muslims	1.6m	3
Hindus	559k	1
Sikhs	336k	0.6
Jews	267k	0.5
Buddhists	152k	0.3
Others	179k	0.3
None (No Religion)	9m	15.3

The following table shows the percentage of people in different age groups in the Muslim, Sikh and Hindu faiths.

Age	All (%)	Muslims (%)	Sikhs (%)	Hindus (%)
0 – 15	20	34	25	21
16 – 24	11	18	17	15
25 – 49	35	37	41	43
50 – 59	13	5	9	10
60 +	21	6	9	11

Birmingham contains a large number of British Muslims. According to the 2001 Census, over 140,000 or 14.3% of a population of about 977,000 described themselves as Muslims. Statistics for religious adherence can be seen in the table below.

	Number of People	Percentage
Christians	577k	59%
Muslims	140k	14.3%
Hindus	29k	2.9%
Sikhs	19k	1.9%
Jews	2.9k	0.3%
Buddhists	2.3k	0.24%
Others	2.5k	0.26%
None (No Religion)	121k	12.4%

It is obligatory for all Muslim men to go to the mosque to read their Friday prayer. For this reason, many mosques are always occupied to their full capacity at this time. Furthermore, two major festivals are celebrated by Muslims; these being Eid-Al-Adha and Eid-Al-Fitr. It has been estimated that on these occasions alone, the number of Muslims that attend the main mosques in Birmingham are approximately 20,000 at the Central Mosque, 16-17,000 at Ghamkol Sharif Mosque in Small Heath and in many other mosque congregations there would be up to 2,000.

Migration and Settlement

Two models can be applied when looking at the settlement of the Muslim community, these being: the Jewish model, where people move and live near a synagogue and the Irish model, where people disperse over a wide area. Muslims in Birmingham are largely connected to a core area which contains Muslim institutions and facilities such as mosques, halal butchers and Muslim schools. However, there is an expansion of Muslim communities where they seem to be moving into areas without these facilities.

The Yemenis were the first settled local Muslim community in the late 1930s. Most of the first Yemeni migrants, who are now mainly elderly men, live in the Balsall Heath area of Birmingham. The second group to arrive were Muslims from Hyderabad, who were older, educated males. After World War II, Muslims from Pakistan arrived followed by adult males, mostly manual labourers, from Azad Kashmir/Mirpur. By the late 1960's East African Asians, including Muslims, arrived in the UK from Kenya and Uganda. In the twenty-first century, Birmingham is home to small communities of Arabs, Iraqi Kurds, Iranians, Afghans, Sudanese, Somalis, Nigerians, Bosnians, Kosovans and Chechnyans. Once settled, male migrants often brought their families to Birmingham.

In order to see the distribution of the Muslim population in Birmingham the best model to use is based on the percentage of Muslim children in primary schools. These figures are constructed from the definitions which parents of primary school children gave of the religious adherence of their children. There are 39 wards in Birmingham, of which 19 have a 0-5% Muslim population, 6 wards have a 5-15% Muslim population, 7 wards have a 15-30% population and 7 wards have a 50+% population of Muslims. The following table shows the percentage of primary school pupils by religion in 2001-2002 in the fourteen wards which contain 15% or more Muslims.

↑ *Dr. Chris Hewer, Special Advisor to the Anglican Bishop of Birmingham.*

Inner City	Christians (%)	Muslims (%)	Sikhs (%)	Hindus (%)
Handsworth	23	60	5	3
Aston	30	55	<1	<1
Nechells	39	52	<1	<1
Washwood Heath	23	72	<1	<1
Small Heath	10	85	<1	<1
Sparkbrook	14	77	2	1
Sparkhill	16	71	3	4
Moseley	63	18	4	1
Ladywood	42	24	6	2
Soho	34	28	16	10
Sandwell	39	15	25	11
Fox Hollies	53	19	3	3
Hall Green	59	18	9	8
Edgbaston	53	15	12	4

BIRMINGHAM

NEW WARD BOUNDARIES JUNE 2004
PROPOSED NEW CONSTITUENCY BOUNDARIES
FROM NEXT GENERAL ELECTION

🔼 *Birmingham City Map [Source: www.birmingham.gov.uk].*

🔼 *Presentation at Birmingham Council House by*
Dr. Chris Hewer to diverse citizens.

It has been estimated that at some time between 2015 and 2020, in terms of ethnicity, Birmingham is likely to be composed of a largely Black/Asian community. This increase will mainly be due to the natural process of people having children and therefore expanding the community. In addition, the size of local Muslim communities is likely to be affected by the presence of asylum seekers and refugees, internal immigration within Europe, for example, Somalis moving from Holland, and local Muslims bringing partners to Birmingham from their country of origin.

Furkhandah J Sindhu

Reference

1. This is an edited version of a presentation by Dr. Chris Hewer, special advisor to the Anglican Bishop of Birmingham.

5

Afghans

The Afghan Community

Afghanistan is a wildly beautiful country in the heart of Central Asia. In the late 1990s, the country held the world's worst records in a number of fields, including infant and maternal mortality, life expectancy, access to safe water, the estimated number of land mines and physically disabled people, those dependent upon food rations, and numbers of refugees. Many Afghan refugees came to Britain. However, Afghanistan's history is not just a story of disorder and deprivation. The country has a rich spiritual and artistic heritage and a diverse culture, language and ethnicity, deriving from centuries of cross fertilisation by different peoples. Afghanistan is comprised of a variety of ethnic groups, Pashtuns (38%), Tajiks (25%), Uzbeks (6%) and the Hazara (19%). The country is further divided along religious lines, Sunni Islam is the dominant faith but there are also Shias within the Hazara and Ismaili minorities. While two Indo-Iranian languages, Dari and Pashto are most widely used, one also encounters Uzbeki, Baluchi, and Nuristani among many others. The capital Kabul, is the most important town, but most people live in villages and engage in agriculture. A significant minority follow a nomadic lifestyle.

Afghanistan gained autonomy from the Persian kingdom of Nadir Shah in 1747, under Ahmad Shah Durrani. After his death, the Durrani Empire began to disintegrate and, as a result, conflicts developed among the various tribes. Yet, the Durrani monarchy managed to retain power until the overthrow of King Zahir Shah. In 1953 Zahir Shah appointed his nephew, Daoud Khan, to the office of Prime Minister. Immediately Daoud began to modernise Afghanistan with the help of Soviet funding. Hoping to halt the growth of Soviet influence the King removed Daoud. Then in 1973, Daoud staged a coup declaring Afghanistan a Republic

with himself as President. Daoud ruled harshly, imprisoning opponents of his government including members of the People's Democratic Party of Afghanistan (PDPA) and Islamists. In April 1978, Daoud himself was killed in a military coup. Internal power struggles, political assassinations and rebellions plunged the country into instability.

Alarmed by the deteriorating situation and the prospect that an anti-communist uprising could threaten to engulf its own southern republics, the USSR mounted a full-scale invasion in 1979. Babrak Karmal was sworn in as the new communist head of state. Babrak denounced the policies of his predecessors and promised to demonstrate respect for Islamic and Afghan traditional values; it was too little too late. Islamist organisations had become the nucleus of the resistance. These guerrilla forces included numerous factions and operated from within the Pakistani city of Peshawar. Suffering almost 50,000 fatalities and caught in an ongoing quagmire, the Red Army finally withdrew its last troops in 1989, having created a huge refugee problem as millions of Afghans fled to Pakistan and Iran. Some also escaped to Europe and the USA. With substantial Soviet assistance, the communist government of Najibullah, elected in 1987, held onto power until April 1992, outliving the Soviet Union itself but eventually collapsing as it ran out of resources. Najibullah relinquished power in favour of the Mujahideen, Islamic warriors, but their calm takeover of Kabul was short lived and Afghanistan plunged into four years of terrible civil war. In the 1990s, the Taliban, led by Mullah Omar, seized power; they were a predominantly Pakhtun (Pushtun) Islamic movement supported from within Pakistan. The Taliban aimed to restore stability and enforce Islamic law. In areas under their control, Taliban authorities enforced their version of religious law, enacting policies prohibiting women from working, carrying out corporal punishment for those convicted of certain crimes and discriminating against the country's Shia population. In addition there was a practice of targeting suspected individuals with links with former Soviet-backed governments, the Mujahideen parties, as well as intellectuals, liberals and moderates. During this period, Afghanistan was isolated from outside influences. Much of the country's historical, educational and economic infrastructure was destroyed leading to starvation, disease and a massive refugee problem. The events led to an increasing number of Afghans fleeing to Iran and Pakistan and seeking asylum in Europe.

Oral history interviews conducted with Afghans in Birmingham have confirmed the complexity of the ethnic background of Afghans and the variety of reasons why they left their country: extreme poverty, war, political and ethnic persecution and imprisonment. Most are young men who came during the Taliban era, though there are older Afghans who arrived in the 1980s or early 1990s. Most came to Britain via Pakistan, but Pakistan was only a staging post in the routes to the west. The country was a deeply unsafe place during the Taliban era, given the presence of supporters of the Taliban. They were attracted to Britain because of its reputation for political stability, democracy and educational and employment opportunities.

Experiences within Birmingham have varied greatly. Asylum seekers during the Taliban era were initially housed in hostels and then found accommodation in flats and houses in inner-city Birmingham and the Black Country. Like asylum seekers and refugees from other communities, they report incidents of abuse and physical attack. Most have been keen to improve their English. Many Afghans have experienced problems of adjustment within a western and secular culture with a different social structure and approach to family relationships. There are several community associations which reflect the ethnic and political allegiances in Afghanistan.

Many Afghans have been able to make new lives for themselves, particularly if they have been in Britain for some time. One example is Temur Shah, a member of the Pushtun majority,

The late Dost Muhammad Khan – A Pathan.

who was born in Jalalabad in 1972. He remembers the Soviet invasion and his father's opposition to the Russians. As a boy the school system began to break down and he joined the Mujahidin resistance fighters at the age of fourteen. After the Russians left in 1989 the resulting civil war plunged the country into further

Iranian Art.

chaos. Following his brother, Temur came to England and was granted refugee status. He studied, qualified for university and enrolled on an electronic engineering course at the University of East Anglia. After graduating he worked in ICT and became a designer with a local multinational engineering company.

The recent war in Afghanistan has removed the Taliban from power. Since then it has been virtually impossible for Afghan asylum seekers to secure leave to remain in Britain.

Jahan Mahmood

References

1. Dick, Malcolm, *Celebrating Sanctuary: Birmingham and the Refugee Experience 1750-2002* (Birmingham, Refugee Action, 2002).
2. Dupree, L, *Afghanistan*, (Princeton University Press, 1980).
3. *Encarta Encylopaedia*, various editions (Microsoft Corporation).
4. Fullerton, *The Soviet Occupation of Afghanistan* London (Far Eastern Economic Review, 1984).
5. Gupta, B S, Afghanistan (London, Francis Pinter, 1986).
6. Khan, J, *The Taliban: the Role of USA, UN and Pakistan* (Karachi, Pakistan, Karachi Bookstores, 2000).
7. Maley, W, *Fundamentalism Reborn? Afghanistan and the Taliban* (London, Hurst and Co, 2001).
8. Mahmood, Jahan, *Afghans in Birmingham: a Case Study of a Refugee Community* (Centre for Lifelong Learning, University of Birmingham, BA Dissertation, 2003).
9. Marsden, P, *The Taliban War, Religion and the New Order in Afghanistan* (London, Zed Books, 1998).
10. Roy, O, *Islam and Resistance in Afghanistan* (Cambridge University Press, 1986).

6

Albanians

The Albanian Community

Albanians in Britain, who originate from the Balkans in south-eastern Europe, share a common Albanian national identity which goes back thousands of years. However, their political and religious history has been affected by the experience of conquest by foreign powers and the different influences of Christianity, Islam and Communism.

The Albanian community does not have a long history in Britain. A few young Albanians arrived in the UK shortly after the end of Communism in Albania, mainly to study. The number of Albanians increased from the mid-1990s onwards, most of them coming from Kosova, which was part of the Serbian dominated Yugoslavia. Many Albanians from Albania proper also came to Britain. Albanians in the UK can be classified into three main groups: economic immigrants, asylum seekers and students. The first group includes most of the Albanians coming from the Republic of Albania. In the wake of the collapse of the fraudulent pyramid schemes in Albania in 1997, many Albanians lost their life savings and faith in the country's political elite. Many people of all ages and from all walks of life managed to come to Britain. The second group comprises mainly the Kosova Albanians most of whom were forced to leave their country as a result of the repression exerted by the Serbian regime of President Milosovic over the last two decades of the twentieth century, a policy which culminated in 1999 into the first state–sponsored genocide and ethnic cleansing in Western Europe since the end of the World War II. The third group includes a considerable number of students and scholars who are enrolled and employed at academic institutions in the UK.

Most of the British people would identify the Albanians in this country with the Kosova Albanians. The Kosova conflict has its roots in the decision of the Six European Great Powers at the London Conference in 1913 to dismember the Albanian nations in the wake of the collapse of the Turkish Ottoman Empire, under the false pretext that the Albanians were Muslims and as such not proper Europeans.

The Albanians are the direct descendants of the Illyrians and one of the oldest European nations. Their recorded history predates that of Ancient Greece by almost a millennium. By the end of the third century, the Albanians were one of the first European people to convert to Christianity. Following their defeat by the Romans in 169 BC, except for some short periods, over the past two thousand years, Albanians have lived mostly under foreign rule. From the fifteenth century onwards, like most of the Balkans, Albanian territory was targeted by the Ottoman Turks who eventually came to rule the region for almost five centuries. Following the death of the Albanian national hero Gjergj Kastrioti Skanderbeg, the leader of a long, successful resistance (1443-1468), the Turks suppressed Albanian independence. Towards the end of the fifteenth century, over half a million Albanians left their country, with most of them heading for Italy. Some Albanians had already converted to Islam but others were subject to various forms of pressure to change their religion after the Turks suppressed Albanian independence. Some Albanian Christians saw an advantage in becoming Muslims. Their new religion provided them with an opportunity to join the Turkish administration in the Ottoman Empire despite their ethnic origins. It is believed that some twenty-five Ottoman prime ministers were of Albanian origin.

In the nineteenth century, the Ottoman Empire's hold on the Balkans broke down. Different independent or semi-independent nations emerged and Serbia, a Christian country, became the most powerful of these new states. The Serbian ultra-nationalist Orthodox Church often used the Albanians' conversion to Islam to justify Serbia's colonization of Albanian lands, including the region of Kosova. The Serbs saw Kosova as part of greater Serbia, their 'promised land'. In the late twentieth century, in the former Communist Yugoslav Republic, the Albanians were treated as second-class citizens, not for religious reasons, but because they were not members of the dominant ethnic group, the Slavs. The Kosova issue has never been directly a religious issue, but a national one. Differences between Christianity and Islam have not been a cause of strife amongst Albanians themselves. They are, however, very proud of their Albanian identity.

It is estimated that some 50,000 Albanians are currently living in the UK, 4,000 of them in the West Midlands. The first Albanians settled in Birmingham in 1997. A year later they established their own association. Initially, the association was set up with the purpose of collecting aid for the people of Kosova. The first community worker was appointed in 2001. The association has some 1,500 members. The community worker and volunteers offer help with immigration issues, benefits, housing, education and employment. More recently the association supported an initiative to start classes in Albanian for five to seven year-old children. The classes are run by two qualified female teachers who at the moment do the work for free. The association organises several sport and cultural events throughout the year. A community worker for women would enable many Albanian housewives to integrate better into British society.

The majority of the Albanians have settled well in the West Midlands and most speak very good English. Some have started their own small businesses across the region. Many educated Albanians have found good employment. A large number of the Albanians have been naturalised as British citizens or have been granted permanent residence. Many of them, however, are still waiting to hear the outcome of their applications for leave to remain in the UK and a considerable number have had their applications turned down by the Home Office. It is estimated that 20% of the Albanian community have been refused leave to remain in the country. Some of them have been living and working in Britain as law-abiding citizens and tax-payers almost for a decade. Among this group of Albanians one can find university graduates who are currently working in the black market as manual workers. An amnesty by the British government would enable many highly qualified Albanian nurses, doctors and teachers to offer a much welcome contribution to our under-staffed health service and education system.

The majority of the Albanians in Britain are hard working, decent, law-abiding citizens. The Albanian community in this country deserves to be treated more sympathetically by the British media which often resort to stereotyping, tabloidisation and sensationalisation of those communities which are not properly organized or articulate enough to promote their values.

Gëzim Alpion

References

1. Alpion, Gëzim, *Mother Teresa, the Media and Sainthood* (London, Routledge, 2006).
2. Alpion, Gëzim. "Images of Albania and Albanians in English literature: from Edith Durham to J. K. Rowling' (Paper presented at the Institute for Advanced Research in Arts and Social Sciences at the University of Birmingham, UK, on 12 February 2002). *BESA Journal* (Truro, UK) ISSN:1366-8536 Vol.6 No.2 Spring 2002:30-34.
3. Alpion, Gëzim, Interviews conducted with representatives of the Albanian community in the West Midlands on 11 and 12 July 2005.

4. Cutrilovic, Vaso, "The Expulsion of the Albanians", 7 March 1937. www.aacl.com/expulsion23.html.

5. Kola, Paulin, *The Search for Greater Albania* (London, Hurst & Company, 2003).

6. Durham, Edith, *High Albania* (London, Virago, 1985)

7. *The Holy Bible, Containing the Old and New Testaments with Apocryphal/Deuterocanonical Books*. New Revised Standard Version (New York and Oxford, Oxford University Press, 1989).

8. Prifti, Kristaq, et. al. (eds), *The Truth on Kosova* (Tirana, Encyclopedia Publishing House, 1993).

9. "Serbian Academy of Arts and Sciences Memorandum", September 1986. www.ess.uwe.ac.uk/Kosovo/Kosovo-Background17.htm

10. Malcolm, Noel, *Kosovo: A Short History* (London, Papermac, 1998).

7

Bangladeshis

The Bangladeshi Community

Birmingham is one of the main places of settlement for British Bangladeshis, most of whom can trace their origins to one region in the country, Sylhet. Bangladesh was part of Bengal within British India until 1947, when it became the eastern component of the new state of Pakistan. In 1971, following a civil war, Bangladesh broke away from Pakistan and became an independent state.

The presence of Bangladeshis in Britain dates from the days of the British Empire, when Sylhetis served as seamen on British ships, particularly during World War II. Stranded without work in England, they looked for employment. Birmingham was an obvious choice, given the prosperity of the local economy until the 1970s. The first migrants were employed as unskilled or semi-skilled workers in Birmingham's manufacturing industry and settled in Handsworth, Aston and elsewhere. These areas contained cheap housing where single men and families could live in privately rented or owner-occupied property.

Birmingham's recession in the 1970s and 1980s reduced work opportunities considerably. Lacking fluency in English, educational qualifications and training, many found it difficult to compete in a contracting job market. One response was to seek employment in catering. The 'Indian' restaurants which entered every high street were usually created, managed and staffed by Bangladeshi men. Bangladeshis like other groups have experienced layers of deprivation, but institutions, such as mosques, women's groups, community centres and youth groups have provided identity and support.

The first mosque specifically for the Bangladeshi community was created from a converted dwelling house in Aston in the 1950s, which became the Masjid-E-Noor Mosque. Increasingly mosques have become venues for transmitting culture as well as religion with supplementary schools teaching Islam and the Bengali language to children who were born in Britain.

One stereotype of Asian women portrays them as deferential, home-based and reluctant to seek educational qualifications. Yet Bangladeshi women in Birmingham have secured advanced qualifications, entered professional occupations and created support networks for their community. There have been several active local organisations created by and for Bangladeshi women since the 1970s. The UK Asian Women's Centre in Handsworth, for example, supports those with learning disabilities, provides employment advice and runs a mental health project supported by the local Health Authority and Social Services.

⬆ *Turkish art of illuminated painting, based on antique patterns [Courtesy of COL Cards].*

Local Bangladeshis have developed organisations to provide project activities, support, advice and social facilities. Together they have contributed to raising educational attainment, improving leisure opportunities and skills development in local areas. The Bangladesh Multipurpose Centre in Aston has developed projects to provide support to local elders, enhance careers advice and employment opportunities, establish a supplementary school for children and offer English as a Second Language courses and IT training for adults. Working in partnership with local government, educational institutions and other agencies, it has played a role in regenerating local communities in Aston.

The Bangladeshi Youth Forum (BYF) was created in 1994 and moved into premises in Lozells in 1997. Managed by young people, the BYF has provided leisure opportunities and addressed social exclusion and discrimination. It has offered employment advice and encouraged young people to continue their education. Courses in English as a Second Language and Information Technology have enabled progression to college. Activities have included long-distance cycling expeditions and a trip where sixteen participants visited Belgium, Holland and Germany investigating youth projects on the continent. A joint residential visit was organised with Handsworth Methodist Youth Club to the Malvern Hills, enabling young people from different communities to share experiences.

Malcolm Dick

References

1. Bangladeshi Youth Forum, *Annual Reports*.
2. Bangladeshi Women's Employment Resource Centre, Miscellaneous publications.
3. Birmingham City Council, *Community Profiles: Bangladeshi* (Birmingham City Council, 1995).
4. Birmingham International Council, "BIC President's Evening (31 March 2001): Birmingham and Bangladesh" *The BIC Newsletter* (May 2001).
5. Choudhury, Sabia, *Bangladeshi Women in Birmingham* (Centre for Lifelong Learning, University of Birmingham BA Dissertation, 2002).
6. Choudhury, Yousuf and Drake, Peter, *From Bangladesh to Birmingham* (Birmingham City Council (Birmingham City Council, 2001).
7. Dick, Malcolm, Interviews with members of the Bangladeshi Community conducted in 2004.
8. Millennibrum Project, Video Interviews conducted with individuals at the Bangladeshi Women's Employment Resource Centre, 2001 (Local Studies and History, Birmingham Central Library).

⬆ *Tozammel Huq (circled) with Chaudury Zaman, Abdul Majid, Saleem Javid and AR Mahmood.*

Tozammel Huq: Teacher, Activist and Ambassador

Tozammel, popularly known as Tony, came over in the 1960s from what was then East Pakistan and is now Bangladesh. His family had a tradition of political activism. From a very early age he was active in student politics. He was seen as a thorn in the side of the establishment. On one occasion he was treated as a *security prisoner* for a period of six months. He had the privilege of sharing prison with many figures who were later to become national leaders such as Presidents and Prime Ministers. The main driving force for Tozammel has always been his desire for a more just and fair society. This goes back to his childhood, when, although he himself came from a wealthy family, he saw poverty and deprivation in his neighbourhood.

During the 1960s, when he was in his 20s, in his role as the president of the National Union of Students of Pakistan, he left for Canada to attend a student conference. He came to the UK to study law. His ambition was to go back and serve his country after finishing his Bar examinations. Because of his anti-establishment views and his political activism his family were not allowed to send money to support him in his studies which forced him to work in order to support himself. This is how he entered the teaching profession. His first job was as a supply teacher in Birmingham. Later he was promoted to the position of Headteacher of an inner city school in the city. At that time he was probably one of the first Asian people to be appointed to such a position.

By this time he had also been able to establish himself as a community activist. Soon after arrival in the UK he was elected the national Chairperson of the National Federation of Pakistani Associations, which was an umbrella organisation. Later he founded the Pakistani Workers Association and then, when East Pakistan became Bangladesh in 1972, he founded the Bangladeshi Workers Association. Through such activism, he began to play a central role in the anti-racist movement at this time, working in partnership with not only his own Pakistani/Bangladeshi community but also the other ethnic minority communities and a range of individuals and organisations from the White community. His early anti-racist activity included involvement in the Black People's Alliance which had been set up after the "Rivers of Blood" speech by Enoch Powell and in the struggles during the 1970s.

After six years as a Headteacher he left to take up a post as the Ambassador for the Bangladesh Government to France, Spain and then UNESCO. Later, he did a stint as an Education Adviser with Birmingham City Council. He is currently a Non-Executive Director for the University Hospital Birmingham and an Honorary Research Fellow for the University of Warwick. He has been awarded an Honorary Doctorate by the University of Birmingham and an MBE for services to education.

Tozammel believes that each individual is unique with their own potential which they must work hard to maximise. His advice to young people is: "to have a focus and clear goals and in order to achieve those goals they need determination and perseverance and, above all, hard work" He recalls the advice of one of his own teachers in East Pakistan which he would happily pass onto young people: "Life is not a bed of roses; it always has ups and downs; there are always struggles. But you must not give up or give in".

Karamat Iqbal

Reference

1. www.emaonline.org.uk

Mohammed Hussain:
the transition from University to work

Having finished university I was faced with the daunting task of deciding what to do next, what to do in June, July and August and what to do with the rest of my life. I was so used to being a student and now, suddenly, I no longer was. I needed to find out exactly what I wanted to do, what direction I wanted to take and how to take it. One thing I was quite sure about was that I wanted to do something purposeful, something that would make a difference and something I could build upon.

I finally decided on a temporary post with Birmingham Local Education Authority. Working for the LEA as a researcher on the Raising the Achievement of Pakistani and Bangladeshi Boys Project (RAPBB) was a very exciting and interesting experience, as the research has given me the opportunity to learn more about the root causes of underachievement in the very environment and communities I myself come from. Also, having given teaching serious consideration at university, this was just the type of work which would give me valuable insight into, not only the teaching profession, but also secondary education, on a number of different levels.

The first few weeks were the most difficult. The hardest part was probably adapting to other people relying on me, which makes each and every appointment, meeting and task twice as important. But when I'm enjoying my work and things are constantly busy, I forget to find things difficult and end up just getting on with it.

There have been many different highlights in the last thirteen months. Certain aspects of the work have been eye opening and different. It felt peculiar at first working with people of all ages. I've always associated with my own age group – as a student I suppose most of us inevitably do – but I now found myself addressing people I would have referred to as "Sir", a few years previously, by their first names, which definitely felt strange and weird. I finally came to the complete realisation that teachers were not a different race, creed or kind, but, in fact quite normal and human like me. I began to realise that education, teaching and learning does not start and finish in the classroom. I now had a greater appreciation and understanding for so much more that goes on behind the scenes, things I used to take for granted, things I never ever would have imagined or given a second thought.

I have now reached a resolution that my future lies in education. Whichever sphere I enter this experience has been a self-discovery. It has helped me to make important choices and decisions about my future. I no longer feel like I am facing an immense jungle with a million routes at my disposal, without any knowledge of the most appropriate course to take. I now have a picture, even if a hazy one, which definitely narrows the possibilities.

Yousuf Choudhury and
Britain's Bangladeshi Heritage

When Yousuf Choudhury was born in 1928, he was a citizen of Britain's Indian Empire. His place of birth was Sylhet, a largely agricultural district of East Bengal which became part of the new Muslim state of Pakistan in 1947. In 1971, East Bengal or East Pakistan, as it became known, achieved independence as Bangladesh. Sylhet was a poor area, there was little work for local people so many young men found employment in Britain's Merchant Navy where they sailed the seas importing and exporting goods. They worked for low wages and in poor conditions, but frequently their ships came into British ports. This gave them an opportunity to leave and seek work in better paid industrial employment. In 1957, Yousuf Choudhury came to Birmingham to join and replace his elderly uncle who was his family's main breadwinner. The city was already home to a sizeable number of Bengalis who were employed as labourers in local metal foundries. By English standards their wages were not high, but they were able to send money they had saved back home to their families.

By the early 1960s, Yousuf had settled in Birmingham. He developed a keen interest in photography, turned semi-professional and established a studio in his house. As well as taking portrait images, he also began to photograph the daily lives of his fellow Bengalis. The 1960s also witnessed growing tension between East and West Pakistan as Bengalis sought to create their own country. Yousuf Choudhury identified with this movement and photographed the pro-independence meetings and demonstrations by Bengalis in Britain. In 1971, East Pakistan declared independence and became Bangladesh. During the short-lived war with the central government in Pakistan, law and order and communications broke down and Yousuf lost contact with his daughter, Rohina, who was staying with relatives. Desperate to bring her home, he flew to India, crossed the border into Bangladesh and travelled from village to village to find her. Luckily she was safe and he was able to return to Birmingham with her. On his arrival, he attracted a lot of media attention. The human story of a father's rescue of his daughter was widely reported in newspapers and on the radio. During his search for Rohina, Yousuf had also photographed the sufferings of his countrymen and women. In 2004, a selection of these photographs was published in *An Album of the 1971 Bangladeshi Liberation Movement*.

Towards the end of his life, Yousuf's desire to chronicle the Bangladeshi experience grew. Not only did he take photographs, he also began to record the lives of Bangladeshis who had left their homeland to settle in Britain. The first results were published in 1993 as *The Roots and Tales of the Bangladeshi Settlers*. This book told the stories of the first Bengali settlers in the UK and vividly relates how they lived in cold and overcrowded boarding houses, sleeping in shifts and the forming of relation-ships between men and local women. Another book, *Sons of Empire* (1995), was based on interviews with Bengalis who had served on British ships in two World Wars. Yousuf also turned his attention to the development of the restaurant trade where Bengalis had made a huge contribution. He visited restaurants throughout the UK and the results were published in 2002 as *The Book of Indian Subcontinental Cooking in Britain*.

When Yousuf Choudhury died in 2002, he had shown why Bangladeshis had come to Britain, the ways in which they had contributed to its economy and culture and how they had contributed to the country's fight for survival in World War II. He was proud of his identity and wanted British Bangladeshis to be proud of their heritage and values as well. His publications and the records he created are a pioneering example of what determined individuals and community history can achieve.

Malcolm Dick

References

1. The material for this article has largely been based on a documentary film about Yousuf Choudhury by Makhbul Choudhury. A DVD, *A Son of Empire: A Documentary on Yousuf Choudhury* (Bangla Connection Production, 2004) can be obtained by contacting: banglaconnection@yahoo.co.uk.

2. Local Studies and History on Floor 6 of Birmingham Central Library holds a collection of many of Yousuf Choudhury's original photographs. Birmingham Library Services has also published a summary of the local Bangladeshi experience, jointly written by Yousuf Choudhury and Peter Drake called *From Bangladesh to Birmingham* (Birmingham City Council, 2001).

Identity and Cultural Heritage

What do we mean when we talk of identity? And what does it mean to be a British Bangladeshi? What are the obstacles we need to overcome in order to better define ourselves and to better understand the world around us?

We are living in a continually changing world that brings with it a whole host of uncertainties. Our identities are crucial for grounding us as individuals within our immediate social and cultural environments. Our identities ought to provide us with a sense of place and belonging – of an association with that world – an association that, in turn, enables the community to engage more meaningfully with the wider society.

Our identities therefore need to be responsive to the contemporary world and to draw upon the immediate history and experience of our community in its setting. If not, an identity can become an anachronism – disempowering us when it should be a source of confidence and agency.

To attempt to discuss what it means to be a British Bangladeshi would need far more expansive consideration than is possible here. However, I would stress that what is necessary at this time is a progressive re-engagement with the sources of knowledge that would serve to underpin our understanding of the world around us and our presence within it.

These sources of knowledge are firstly represented by the memories of previous generations. These memories indicate the experiences and the achievements of parents, grandparents, and uncles as they settled in Britain. Secondly, these sources of knowledge are the archives, museums and the libraries that house an extraordinary – though much under-explored – body of knowledge.

Drawing on the first, the lack of dialogue between generations has led to an overall deficit in social and cultural knowledge. Present younger generations are thus disembodied from an immediate past that should have better defined and shaped their identities. This has the affect of disempowering the community when our identities should have been the foundations upon which individuals become active citizens.

To draw on the second, any effort to engage mainstream sectors such as Archives and Museums would be an attempt to re-engage with the wider society and would serve to overcome, in some part, the insularity that leads to isolation. Critically, isolation leads to a limiting of opportunity. To re-engage is to open newer horizons. We need only to look at the significant under-representation of minority communities within the Cultural sector to see how limited our options have been to date.

It is important that we understand the processes that bring us all to where we are. It is also important that the Bangladeshi community begins to actively promote to its members the value in engaging with mainstream sectors and the need to strive forward with progressive agendas and a genuine concern to benefit all communities. This said, it is crucial that mainstream sectors do more to meaningfully engage communities. The diversification of workforces is paramount and increases the potential for cultural provision to reach further and deeper out into communities currently starved of valuable cultural opportunities.

Dealing with the marginalisation – and the considerable lack of opportunity that it brings – requires work on many different fronts. In our efforts to combat under-achievement in education, to train the unemployed and to empower communities, it is important not to forget that Culture is indeed a powerful mechanism for learning, achievement and progress.

There are numerous opportunities to engage on this front. The heritage sector is buoyant with opportunity. Many communities have established projects – others are in the process of developing ideas. But again, there is a distinct lack of a progressive Bangladeshi presence in this sphere of activity. This is set against the backdrop of a sector where funding bodies are struggling to source viable project ideas, and particularly from those communities still under-represented. Where the Bangladeshi community is concerned, there are difficult challenges still to be overcome – some of them, unfortunately, from within.

The Community needs to access existing initiatives designed to enable such incursions into the sector. In Birmingham 'Connecting Histories', a two-year archives project, is one such natural point of entry. The Project has been working to empower community groups in a number of ways; for example, by helping groups to develop ideas, orientating them towards funding streams, and offering valuable volunteering opportunities as a means of transferring skills and experience – all of this demonstrating how partnerships are an important facet of project development and realisation.

This is just one model of engagement. There are others we can look to. In the museums sector there is now a well established programme of Positive Action Traineeships (PATs) under the 'Diversify' programme. The archives sector has just recently followed suit with two PATs created through the 'Connecting Histories' Project. Indeed, my own career is indebted to both of these initiatives. These are significant efforts to redress imbalances within the respective workforces – initiatives that

the Bangladeshi community ought to be orientating some of its young talent towards.

However, in Birmingham, this would require a more concerted approach than has been previously visible. Invariably, opportunities to develop talent will always exist. And the need and desire for projects that communicate all of our heritages and identities – especially in a rapidly transforming and increasingly diverse society – will be ever present. It is therefore a question of how the Bangladeshi Community can respond both to these opportunities and to these challenges. Only after there has been a progressive and genuine engagement with these issues can the Community begin to help its younger members build conceptual frameworks they can use incisively to develop a sense of place and belonging; to help construct identities that are enabling and empowering rather than fuelling discontent and disillusionment.

Izzy Mohammed

Reference

1. Connecting Histories, Floor 3 Central Library, Chamberlain Square, Birmingham B3 3HQ. Tel: 0121 464 1607. E-mail: Connecting.Histories@birmingham.gov.uk.

8

Bosnians

The Bosnian Community

Bosnia is one of the successor states of the former Yugoslavia. Its capital is the city of Sarajevo and the country is made up of a diverse society of Christians, Muslims and Jews. 1992 marked the start of the war in Bosnia-Herzegovina when a Serb sniper allegedly shot two Bosnians who took part in a peace march to support the country's independence. The conflict that followed killed thousands and destroyed much of the country's economy. Bosnians of all communities suffered in the conflict, but the Muslim population experienced 'ethnic cleansing', inflicted by the Serbian authorities, led by the former President of Yugoslavia, Slobodan Milosovic and Bosnian Serb leaders,

Radovan Karadzic and Ratko Mladic. In total 200,000 people died in the conflict. Two million people were made homeless and many were imprisoned in concentration camps or experienced serious injury.

Birmingham is home to about a thousand Bosnians who left the country in three ways. The first came in 1992-93 under a programme called 'Governmental 1000'. This brought survivors of concentration camps to the UK. A second group were evacuees who were injured or paralysed during the war and came to receive medical treatment. Finally there were a small number of refugees who escaped because their homes were destroyed. The newcomers included men and women, families and children and they report that they were received warmly by British people who had been alerted to the horrors of the conflict through the television and other media. The

○ *Young people from various schools participating in a Little Football League in 1989 at Birmingham Sport Centre's Astroturf pitch, near Birmingham Central Mosque.*

Bosnians had temporary leave to remain and were not able to travel, but over time most have gained permanent status in Britain. Their qualifications were not always recognised, so education and training have been central in enabling people to make their way in British society.

Recognising that they cannot live on sympathy, the Bosnian community has engaged in self-help to provide support agencies and maintain their culture. The Bosnia and Herzegovina Refugee UK Network was set up in 1996 with the aim of providing practical and psychological support on behalf of Bosnian refugees in the UK. It is non-sectarian and supports all members of the community whatever their religious background, status, gender or sexuality. The Network's national headquarters is in Birmingham and from its base, the Network produces a monthly newspaper, *Haber*, for the Bosnian community in the UK, which is edited and produced by volunteers. After two years of co-ordination with Bosnian organisations around the world the Network organised the First Conference of the Bosnian Diaspora in Sarajevo in May 2002. This marked the tenth anniversary of the start of the war in Bosnia and occurred in the same year as the Bosnian film maker, Danis Tanovic won the Golden Globe in Los Angeles for the best foreign film, 'No Man's Land'.

Locally advice is provided on housing, health and education. There are translation services and counselling for post-war trauma victims. The Network organises supplementary schools for children with classes in the Bosnian language, art and culture and English. The Network is seeking premises in Birmingham to provide a centre for the community. Like people from other countries, Bosnians in Birmingham have two identities. Their traditional culture inherited from their homeland and their status in Britain where they have secured jobs, made friends and created new lives for themselves.

Malcolm Dick

References

1. Bosnia and Herzegovina Refugee UK "Network" Birmingham, *Haber*, May-June, 2002.
2. Dick, Malcolm, *Celebrating Sanctuary, Birmingham and the Refugee Experience 1750 – 2002* (Refugee Action, 2002).
3. Dick, Malcolm, *Interviews with members of the Bosnian Community conducted in 2002* (Notes in the possession of the author).

9

Iranians

The Iranian Community

Iran, formerly known as Persia, is virtually unknown in Britain. Some people might be able to identify its capital Teheran. Readers of the Bible may know of the warlike Medes and Persians and the visit of the three wise men from the East to the infant Jesus in Bethlehem. In contemporary popular perceptions Iran is associated with fundamentalist Ayattolahs and mullahs, the fatwa against Salman Rushdie and membership of George Bush's 'axis of evil'. These images of Iran reveal little of the culture of a complex, diverse and dynamic society. The country is heir to an ancient history and for centuries has been a major power in the Middle East and Central Asia. The West Midlands is home to a few thousand Iranians, most of whom arrived in the last few years as asylum seekers and refugees to escape from what they saw as a repressive society. Most of them are proud of their country and its rich traditions. Their past is integral to their identity and they are keen to talk about its history and achievements to those who are willing to listen.

Some of the earliest Persian artefacts include metalwork made by the Kassites of East Lorrestan in north western Iran. The Kassites bred horses and produced exquisite bronze horse bits, daggers and domestic items in about 1000 BCE. Under the Achaemenid Dynasty from 550 to 330 BCE, Persia was one of the world's civilisations. The Achaemenids created Persopolis, near Shiraz, one of the great cities of the ancient world, which lay disguised by sand until the 1930s. They also introduced paved roads for horse-drawn vehicles and the world's first pony express mail service.

For over 2,000 years, invasion and cross-fertilisation influenced Persian life. Alexander the Great conquered the country after 330 BCE and the Macedonian Seleucids stamped Greek language and culture upon an older Persian civilisation. The Romans never conquered Persia and after the Seleucids, the country was governed by the nomadic Parthians until a new dynasty, the Sassanians, took over. Greek influence was countered by native influences, but conflict with the Christian Byzantine Empire and other neighbours weakened the country and enabled the Arabs to conquer Persia in the seventh century AD. They introduced Arabic and Islam. Persian Islam was Shi'ite, different from the dominant Arabic Sunni tradition. Most Persians abandoned their traditional religion, Zoroastrianism, but under the Abbasid and Seljuk Dynasties, Persia experienced a period of cultural effervescence. In the early thirteenth century, the Mongol invaders, led by Chinggis Khaan (Genghis Khan) destroyed cities, monuments and documentary records. In the fourteenth century, Farsi replaced Arabic and the Timurid and Safavid Dynasties encouraged miniature painting, translucent tiling, town planning and the building of ornamental mosques, which in turn influenced Turkish and Moghul Indian decorative traditions. Contact and conflict with other countries, the Sunni Ottoman Empire, Portuguese adventurers, English merchants, Afghan invaders and Russian intruders influenced Persian history between the seventeenth and nineteenth centuries.

Iran was never colonised directly by European powers, but the discovery of oil encouraged the Soviet Union, Britain and the USA to intervene in its affairs and attempt to influence its politics in the twentieth century. The Islamic Revolution in 1979, when the Shah of Iran was forced to leave and the Ayatollah Khomeini secured power, was an attempt to revive the Shi'ite Islamic tradition and reject Western, particularly US, influence.

Iran is a diverse, multi-cultural society. There is ethnic and linguistic complexity, represented by the numerically dominant Farsis and others such as Azaris, Kurds, Lors, Arabs, Turkmens and nomads such as the Baluchis and Ghashghaie (Qashqai). Iran has more refugees than any other country in the world, probably in excess of two million in a population of 80 million. They are mainly from Iraq and Afghanistan. Though subject to different constraints and dress codes than men, women are well-educated, participate in music and film making and are represented in the Iranian parliament. There is a long tradition of debate and political pluralism and a vibrant film industry, but religious conservatives are dominant politically and culturally. Though most Iranians are Shi'ite Muslims there are minority Sunni traditions and a small, long-established Christian population, though it is forbidden to convert to Christianity in the country. Other Iranians are Zoroastrians or belong to a more recent faith, the Bahai religion. Tensions between religious conservatives and modernisers, persecution and torture have led several Iranians to leave their country and seek refuge in the West.

↑ *Detail from 'Colourful Dream', oil painting by Iranian Artist, Mohsen Keiany.*

Ali Ahmedpour, a young Iranian in Birmingham, was born in Northern Iran. He went to university, qualified as an accountant and worked for a bank. As a keen cyclist he participated in cycling events. Some members of his family were involved in government and the intelligence service constantly monitored them. Some of them were arrested. Problems were created for him with his employers and he left his job in 1997. He made a living in the export-import business, but was constantly evading the attentions of the political police. He escaped to Turkey and eventually made his way to the UK in 2000. Ebrahim Rashidi came from Azerbaijan in the Northeast of Iran. He went to university, qualified as an accountant and worked in the civil service. He left Iran and came to Britain as an asylum seeker. Meeting Ali in Birmingham, he found that they shared an interest in cycling. Sponsored by the Angel Group, a provider of housing for asylum seekers, Ebrahim and Ali have used their cycling to draw attention to the experience of refugees. Their journeys in 2001 attracted extensive press coverage. By cycling around Britain they promoted positive images of refugees and asylum seekers and drew attention to the difficulties they faced in their own countries and in Britain. Ali and Ebrahim were granted leave to remain in the UK and settled in Birmingham. They are working full-time and are married with families. Ali is employed as a bus driver and Ebrahim works for Birmingham City Council.

Some Iranians have been successful in establishing restaurants, including those providing Iranian cuisine, and fast food outlets, especially pizza shops across the Midlands. Still more have taken advantage of educational opportunities at local colleges, studying English, vocational programmes and Access courses. Several young Iranians are studying ICT at Midlands universities. A local artist, Mohsen Keiany, is a distinguished contributor to artistic life.

Malcolm Dick

References

1. Armstrong, Karen, *Islam: a short History* (London, 2001).
2. Armstrong, Karen, *The Battle for God: Fundamentalism in Judaism, Christianity and Islam*, (London, 2001).
3. Boyle, J A, *Persia, History and Heritage*, (London, 1978).
4. Dick, Malcolm, *Celebrating Sanctuary: Birmingham and the Refugee Experience 1750-2002* (Birmingham, Refugee Action, 2002).
5. Dick, Malcolm, "Introduction" in Keiany, Mohsen, *Conflict and Spirituality: Persian Images of War and Survival. Exhibition Catalogue* (Mohsen Keiany, 2004).
6. Dick, Malcolm, *Interviews with members of the Iranian Community conducted in 2001 – 2005.* (Notes in the possession of the author)
7. Hiro, Dilip, *The Longest War – The Iran-Iraq Military Conflict* (London, 1989).
8. Lewis, Bernard, *The Middle East, 2000 Years of History from the Rise of Christianity to the Present Day* (London, 1995).
9. Regional Surveys of the World, *The Middle East and North Africa*, various editions, (London, various dates).
10. Matheson, Sylvia, *Persia: an Archaeological Guide* (London, 1972).
11. Pope, Arthur Upham, *Introducing Persian Architecture* (London, 1965).
12. Yale, Pat, Ham, Anthony and Greenway, Paul, *Iran* (Victoria, Australia, 2001).

An Iranian Artist in Birmingham

Mohsen Keiany's paintings present Iranian culture to the world, mediated through a personal vision informed by his education, intellect and spirituality. Mohsen was born in Shiraz, one of Iran's most beautiful cities and the urban heartland of Persian civilisation, best represented by the poet Hafez (1324-1389 AD). Mohsen's father, a factory worker, died when he was nine. His mother laboured on a farm to support her four children and despite her poverty paid for him to have a good education. He revealed his artistic talents as a pupil, but the Iran-Iraq War from 1980-1990 disrupted his schooling. Like all young Iranian men he was conscripted. Mohsen served in the army fighting Saddam Hussain's Iraqi invasion. The conflict witnessed trench warfare, poison gas and the killing of 500,000 men on each side by weaponry supplied by the USSR and the West. Mohsen was wounded and saw his friends being mutilated and murdered by modern military hardware. His experience in the conflict has influenced the emotional content of much of his art.

On his return home Mohsen completed his high school education, became a teacher and married. His abilities enabled him to gain a scholarship to university to study art, secure a master's degree and qualify to teach as a lecturer in higher education. His education provided a broad introduction to both eastern and western artistic traditions from prehistory to the present, which are illustrated with effect in his paintings. He showed his paintings in national and international exhibitions and won prizes and taught art history at the University of Shiraz.

In 2000 Mohsen left Iran and arrived in England. In Birmingham he restarted his career as an artist and teacher and exhibited widely. His work ranges from illustrations for children's books to cartoons and multi-media paintings.

Mohsen's paintings integrate different styles to produce works with many religious, historical, psychological and social

⬆ *Mohsen Keiany's portrait by John Davenport RBSA (www.jdportraits.co.uk).*

meanings. They can convey inward contemplation, the harmonious relationship between man and the natural world, human suffering and the horrors of war. The traditions of Persian miniature painting and architecture as well as western movements such as Expressionism and Surrealism infuse his work. Mohsen's inspiration also comes from Iranian archaeology, Persian mythology, the country's landscape, Islam and other world religions. Sufi Mysticism is a special influence. It is a fascinating exercise analysing his paintings to identify their historical and cultural influences and spiritual and psychological meanings.

Malcolm Dick

Why I became an Artist

That special day when I was born was cold, dark, foggy and gloomy. All the roads to the small village were blocked by snow and on her own my mother gave me life. She thought I would never survive, but I was lucky.

I was nine when the Islamic Revolution happened. The only things that I remember were demonstrations against the Shah, shooting, explosions, screaming voices and bloodshed. The Imam of the local mosque showed photographs of dead bodies to encourage us to protest against the Shah. I was ten when my father, the only person who always encouraged me to paint, died. It was a big shock to me. I did not want to accept the truth of my father's death. I used to escape from people.

When the Iran-Iraq war happened, I was eleven and the war preoccupied my mind. It was not the only war that I knew something about. Persian history is full of the anguish of war.

My father used to tell me about these wars and how many times my motherland was deformed by enemies such as Alexander, the Arabs, Genghis Khan, Timur and many others.

I grew up in a culture of fighting. When I was thirteen the fever of war was very high. All the television programmes were dominated by war news and this affected our minds. I left high school aged fourteen and went to the front line, with many other classmates.

My senses were drenched by explosions, shooting, bullets, voices, the reek of gunpowder, intolerable heat and dry sand. My best friend's face was shattered, he held onto my arms and I waited for his last breath. Wounded soldiers begged for help with their eyes. I walked on dead bodies. Everywhere there were screams, bleeding, the smell of garlic, chemical bombs and gas masks. My friends were gassed, rolling on the hot sand and dying like fish out of water. I was injured three times but survived. My mother prayed for me all the time.

I was a soldier for more than two years. War finished when I was seventeen. I came back home from war but was a stranger to everyone, even my mother. I became mentally ill. My doctor was a simple Sufi and painting became my medication. He gave me a spiritual prescription and wanted me to record my memories in paint and share them with other people.

Mohsen Keiany

Reference

1. Keiany, Mohsen *Conflict and Spirituality: Persian Images of War and Survival. Exhibition Catalogue* (Mohsen Keiany, 2004).

10

Pakistanis and Kashmiris

Pakistani Community

People from the Indian sub-continent have been travelling to Britain from as early as the 17th century and Pakistanis, from the north-west of the subcontinent, are now the third largest ethnic minority group in Britain. The migration of people from Pakistan to Britain took place in the 1950s and the 1960s, when government and industry encouraged migration from the former colonies to satisfy its manpower needs after the Second World War. Many Pakistanis were economic migrants from rural areas of the country and most came with a view to return to Pakistan once they had made enough money in Britain. Throughout the 1960s and 1970s their numbers increased. During the 1950s and 1960s most Pakistanis became factory workers. Men came over first and then wives, children and dependants followed. Most of the Pakistanis who came to Birmingham were from the Mirpur district in Kashmir. However others were from areas such as Campbellpur, Nowshera and Gujrat, Rawalpindi, Multan, Faisalabad, Sailkot, Vahari, Burawala and Lahore.

By the 1960s and 1970s many Pakistanis believed it would be difficult to return home due to various factors. These included higher living standards in the UK, the need to maintain new businesses, the presence of children in the school system and political instability in Pakistan. Therefore the community stayed and grew. In Birmingham, Balsall Heath was a popular area to live. It was close to factories where men worked and housing was cheap.

Homes were often shared between different households and over-crowding, cramped living conditions and lack of adequate sanitary provision was common. Many families tolerated such housing conditions due to an inability to afford anything better.

One survey showed 32% of households were overcrowded. This was often due to the high number of children and relatives living as a family unit.

The 1991 and 2001 census returns found that 80% of the community was concentrated in the inner city areas of Small Heath, Sparkhill, Sparkbrook, Washwood Heath, Alum Rock and Nechells. Other areas where the community has made its home were Aston, Handsworth, Moseley, Kings Heath, Edgbaston, Hall Green and Ladywood.

As the first wave of immigrants had a background of little, if any, proper educational qualifications, they became factory workers. With the decline of the manufacturing industries in the city during the 1980s, many Pakistanis became unemployed. By 1991 56% of men had no earned income. Some of the community became self employed. Retail businesses were started, often involving the whole family. Businesses such as travel agents, chemists and jewellers sprang up in Balsall Heath's Ladypool Road, Stratford Road, Green Lane in Small Heath and the Alum Rock Road in Saltley. Many private mini-cab firms were started, leading to most inner-city cabbies being Pakistani. Of course the most famous businesses were the Balti restaurants.

Education of the children was always important to families. Some state schools were seen as educationally poor and sometimes Muslim values were not maintained. This led to the setting up of private education in specialist schools, where Islamic values were taught. By 1991 there were three of these schools in the city. However, some second or third generation children of the original factory workers have done well out of the state education system and a growing number have become professionals in the fields of medicine, teaching, community work and local government.

Throughout the inner city, mosques were either built or adapted from private houses. They became a hub of community

⬆ *Ladypool Road. Ladypool is often referred to as the Balti Triangle as it houses over 50 restaurants. These encompass both Indian and Pakistani cuisine. Baltis have become the nation's favourite dish – a traditional curry with aromatic spices, fresh herbs and tantalising masalas. In addition it accommodates cultural shops, which specialise in Asian clothes and fashion, as well as Bollywood merchandise. The flags posted on various locations provide a sense of pride, whilst celebrating community cohesion.*

life by providing religious instruction to the young, educating them in Arabic and emerging as social and cultural centres.

The most famous thing the Pakistani community has given us is the Balti. Birmingham is well known for its Balti Belt, a cluster of Balti restaurants packed into inner city Birmingham. This spicy dish was introduced to the city by its large Kashmiri population. It is a way of cooking that started in the city in the 1980s and developed to become a favourite of many a Brummie whatever his culture.

Many young Pakistani boys continue to play cricket and pack out the Edgbaston Cricket Ground whenever the Pakistan side tour England. You can hear the cheers for them outside the ground! The traditional game of *Kabaddi* is also still played.

Several self-help community groups have been founded over the years. *The Pakistan Welfare Association* for example, has been established since the 1950s. Other examples are the Pakistan Youth Forum, the Birmingham Pakistan Sports Forum and the Pakistan Forum. In the political arena Birmingham has also a number of councillors with Pakistani and Kashmiri origins.

From the first wave of immigrants in the 1950s, the Pakistani community has developed and made a significant impact on Birmingham in economic, social, religious, educational and political terms.

Makhdoom Chishti

Reference

1. www.birmingham.gov.uk

The Kashmiri Community

A very large percentage of people of Pakistani origin in Birmingham are from a district known as Mirpur, a region situated in Azad (or liberated) Kashmir in Northern Pakistan. Today, Kashmiris make up the largest ethnic group in Britain after the Irish community. Different Asian communities are dominant in different cities. In Bradford and Birmingham, the Pakistanis are predominant, with possibly more Mirpuris living in Birmingham.

Pakistanis started to arrive in Britain in the 1950s and continued to migrate in the 1960s and 1970s. At first, young males were needed to work in manual occupations following the shortage of workers after the Second World War. Many came with the intention of staying only for a short time. Wages may not have been high, but they were worth a great deal more in their home country than in Britain, so their families benefited from their labour. Many of the first generation of men worked in factories and lived in shared accommodation before earning enough money to obtain their own homes and bring their families from Pakistan. Gradually they laid down roots as their children attended local schools and they bought their own properties and created businesses. The local community flourished by catering for their cultural and religious needs as specialist fabric and spice stores sprang up and mosques were built. As newcomers acquired a greater sense of security, Britain became home and many returned to Pakistan only for an occasional holiday. Away from Pakistan, local Kashmiris made their own impact on Birmingham by inventing the balti, one of Britain's culinary delights.

The Mirpuri community is the Pakistani equivalent to the Sylhetis for Bangladeshis, the Yemenis for the Arabs or the Cantonese for the Chinese. For each nation whose people migrated to the shores of Britain, a large part of their popula-

Adam Yousef (2nd left) with AQ Lodhi and M Ali at an Islamic Stall, outside the Birmingham Central Mosque.

tion came from one single region or district as families and friends followed each other in search of work and a better life. These origins are indicated in the names of travel agents, chemists, newsagents, cornershops, jewellers, green-grocers, supermarkets, mini-cab firms, takeaways and balti restaurants called after hometowns such as Lahore, Karachi, Mirpur, Dadyal and the like.

Communities are focused to a great extent on an identity which is linked to a particular place or social group in Pakistan. Families may disallow marriages and official family links to people from other regions or classes, as if to suggest a person's birthplace can in some way signify their status and standing in the community. Nevertheless, these notions became less potent in Britain than in Pakistan, where it was important for the community as a whole to remain together as a tight-knit unit for the sake of security, identity and belonging. As time passes, younger British Asians are losing the traditional sense of regional and status identity. Today, it is only the more recent immigrants that maintain pride in their titles and districts. Most youngsters, however, only know "Mirpur", "Mirpuri" and "Kashmiri" as words. Occasionally they recall the name at some community gathering such as a wedding when they might be asked about where their father is from by an elder who fought in the British Army in World War Two or by the parents of the bride in a possible arranged marriage.

Many young British Asians see themselves as English Asians, Scottish Asians, Welsh Asians, British Asians or just British. They are influenced by customs which are common to everyone else in the country and, as they move forward in life, they can pick and choose what they want. As ethnic identity becomes less and less important, its imprint on lifestyle appears to lose its influence. In recent years, many young Pakistanis in Birmingham have embraced their religious iden-

↑ *Mirpuri week 22-28 March 2004.*

**Film
Sport
Photography
Workshops
Music
Conference**

tity more than their cultural identity as Mirpuris, so being a Brummie Muslim is usually enough for them. Whether Birmingham's second, third and fourth generations of 'Kashmiris' see themselves as Mirpuri, Pakistani, British or something completely different, one thing is for sure, they are all Brummies.

Adam Yousef

Kalsoom Bashir: Local Solicitor

I see myself as a citizen of Birmingham first and foremost. I attended Broadway School in Perry Barr. My family moved to Erdington and I continued my education at Erdington Girls' School, now Kingsbury School. From there I went on to Higher Education and completed my Law degree in 1991 and subsequently qualified as a solicitor in January, 1995. For the last ten years I have worked as a criminal defence solicitor. Five

years ago, together with others, I set up BMV Solicitors and for the last three years I have been its Principal. BMV Solicitors is a firm specialising in Criminal Law.

I came from a community where traditionally girls did not go to university. The norm was to leave school at the age of sixteen and the expectation was geared towards becoming a wife and mother. I am grateful to my parents who valued education and provided the support I needed to go on to Higher Education. As a result, I was one of the first girls to go to university within my community. It is now the norm to go on to college and beyond. However, it is fair to say that I did not take anything for granted. I maximized every opportunity I was given and worked hard. I strove to achieve my personal best at all times. I was probably guilty of nurturing a healthy competitiveness within my circle of friends. I was fortunate in the peer support I had over the years. One friend in particular, whose life almost mirrored mine, has given me immeasurable support for many years. I still have close ties with friends who are from a mix of cultural backgrounds.

I married in 1995. Because of my husband's open attitude to life, I had the option of combining my traditional role as a wife with my career as a solicitor. I chose to do both.

I focused on the area of law that caught my imagination the most – Criminal Law. As ever, this was not the easy option with its unsocial hours and inherent challenges. Now, as an Asian woman running a busy criminal practice, I look back and feel that I have had to work twice as hard to achieve the same goals. Life as a criminal solicitor is complex. The demands of deadlines, achieving the right results for clients and running a business are amongst the constant challenges. It is often difficult to achieve the balance between home and work life, but I think I have managed the right combination. Inherently the legal profession has significantly fewer women than men in the workforce. This is surprising, given the fact that during my

Law degree course, for example, there were an equal number of women to men. Even today, there are few senior solicitors who are women and even fewer senior solicitors who are Asian women.

I have now been qualified for ten years. I am fortunate to work with committed colleagues at BMV Solicitors and will always be grateful for the unwavering support from my husband, family and friends.

Rabiyah K Latif: A Muslim British Pakistani Woman

I consider myself to be a Muslim British Pakistani Woman. I was born in an average Pakistani, Mirpuri family with the usual background setting of a father coming to England in the 1960's to work and a mother following to support and nurture. Without even realising, time had passed them by and the second generation was already in full flow and growing up in a different world.

Like many young Pakistani women, I had the opportunity to move away from home to go to university and begin my career following my education. London was my destination for a period of almost 7 years. I ventured home at the age of twenty four and soon found myself at the heart of the community again. Having left at eighteen, I had come back a different person.

As time went on I soon began to realise and appreciate that throughout my upbringing I had been exposed to and moulded by three cultures: the Muslim, the Pakistani and the British culture.

British culture had influenced me largely through my education and then my career to become the person I was in a setting external to that of the home and the community in which I belonged. Basic rules and guidance throughout my education and career have equipped me with the necessary tools for interaction in a society where opportunities presented them-selves widely for the taking. I was taking them and still am. The environments I have come to encounter through these settings have shaped the decisions I have made within them, taking into consideration and applying the basic guidance that was provided from the outset.

↑ *Special feature published by the Evening Mail on Islam awareness week. [Source: courtesy of Evening Mail, Friday November 19, 2004].*

Pakistani culture has embedded the traditions of the etiquette of our forefathers which were preserved by our parents to ensure they did not lose their original identity. This has filtered through in the manner whereby I carry on my relations within the community, the language I speak and the clothes I choose to wear within these settings. We have been raised to build together and come together at times of happiness and joy, to support and guide one another and to ensure the outcome would be that of benefit and contentment.

Individual roles and responsibilities are shared within the family. My role as a sister and daughter are clearly defined through traditions that even today are crucial and lived everyday within most families. The role I have come to adopt in the family is that of carer and carrier.

My identity and everyday being as a Muslim, I know, is at the core of this cultural fusion. Its history, ethics, principles and morals tailor my daily actions no matter what the setting. Islam, being the way of life adopted some five hundred years ago, played partner to the Pakistani traditions within which I was raised. My Islamic values are with me no matter where my journey takes me. The setting or role I am playing at any given time will be accompanied with the grounding that Islam provides through its authentic guidance and teachings that are easily applicable today.

Each cultural influence plays a key function in the way I carry myself with good practice taken from each one and used with the common intention to strive. Taking a closer look at the above, though, it soon dawns on me that each cultural influence actually complements the other if used as rightly intended. After all, utilising each cultural influence I have been exposed to in my upbringing is what makes me a Muslim British Pakistani Woman.

Shahista Zamir

I'm quite self-disciplined because in Islam you're not meant to be socialising with the opposite sex, but the thing is it's inevitable because females and males will mix and it's a matter of how you deal with situations. The only way I can deal with situations is not going to parties, because at parties a lot of flirting goes on. There could be drugs or alcohol, things I'm forbidden to take as a Muslim and I adhere to Islamic rules and principles. For example I don't smoke, I don't drink, I don't take drugs, and I don't have relationships with men outside marriage. You can only have a relationship with your husband if you are married and your husband only.

I think a lot of people follow a culture rather than Islam… Our culture is based on Pakistan. I get quite annoyed when I hear that my mum is following Pakistani culture. For example in Pakistani dress you have a see-through scarf on your head, whereas in Islam you're meant to cover your head. So I wear Islamic dress more than Pakistani dress. I wouldn't consider myself Pakistani in the sense that I've never visited the country.

A lot of Muslims don't have television because they feel that it affects their judgement, their children's judgement and their outlook towards life. Islam encourages Muslims to read and to educate themselves, however the television is seen as a negative source portraying violence and nudity and so Muslim parents would prefer their children not to see these sorts of things. My mum and dad have never really stopped us watching television, but whenever, for example, a sex scene comes up we just automatically jump towards the remote and change the channel because we don't watch that kind of thing. We're not meant to in Islam, but what we do is we try making excuses.

I wear a hajib, which basically covers my head. In Islam a woman is only allowed to show her face and her hands and some scholars think that they're not allowed to show their feet. But we don't believe that. We think we can show the feet.... I do keep covered up. I generally wear slightly baggy clothes, nothing that's too tight.

At interviews I am automatically perceived as someone who's quiet, shy and who doesn't talk to people. I get very disappointed about that, because I think that sometimes wearing the hajib limits the amount of jobs I would get if I didn't wear this scarf. When I go shopping in town I don't see many girls wearing the hajib. You don't see someone wearing traditional Islamic dress because they feel that they won't fit in with British society.

Reference

1. This extract from the transcript of an oral history interview with Shahista Zamir was conducted by Helen Lloyd for the Millennibrum Project in 2001, Birmingham City Archives, MS 2255/145. A copy of the original minidisk recording and transcript are available for consultation in Local Studies and History, Floor 6 of Birmingham Central Library.

Choudhury Zaman Ali: A Leader in his Community

Choudhury Zaman Ali was born during the first years of the twentieth century in the village of Kalyal in Mirpur, in what is now the region of Azad Kashmir in Pakistan. He received little formal education and could only speak Mirpuri. Local opportunities for career advancement were not available to a poor, uneducated man from a rural area. When Zaman was growing up, Pakistan was part of Britain's Indian Empire and, like many young Asians, Zaman found employment as a lascar or sailor in the British Merchant Navy.

Sailing the seas might have been the summit of his achievements had not his ship docked in Hull, Yorkshire, at some time during the 1930s. Zaman went for a walk to explore the town, got lost and missed his ship when it left port. He could not speak a word of English, but by some means he found his way to London, even though he did not know anyone there.

London was a place of opportunity. There was plenty of available work and it already possessed a sizeable Asian community. The first MPs from British India had been elected to Parliament in the late nineteenth century. Gandhi and Jinnah had lived in London for a while and the city was home to students and intellectuals who were keen supporters of self-government for British India.

Zaman was not as well-educated as these prominent individuals, so how did he make ends meet? His first job was for an American film company in London which was looking for people who could ride horses. He was lucky and played similar roles in two other films. He managed to save enough money to start a small business, selling goods from door to door. Later in life he looked back on these times: 'English people were very kind, hospitable and considerate and used to show genuine affection and sympathy for foreigners. Things were very cheap indeed. You could live comfortably on 10 shillings a week.'

At some time during his stay in London he became a friend of Krishna Menon (1897–1974), a barrister and a Labour Party councillor for St Pancras from 1934 to 1947. Menon became Secretary of the India League which campaigned for self-government, India's first High Commissioner (ambassador) to Britain between 1947 and 1952, the country's delegate to the United Nations from 1952 to 1962 and its Minister of Defence in the 1960s. Zaman's association with influential British Asians in London helped him to make important contacts and build his confidence.

For reasons we do not really know, Zaman moved to Birmingham in the 1940s, one of the first men of Pakistani origin to settle in the city. Birmingham was a relatively prosperous place during and after the Second World War and there was plenty of work for the industrious and ambitious. At a party, he met his future wife Margaret, who came from Scotland. Margaret later told a journalist of her first impressions: 'It was love at first sight. At the time I never realised that the person I was falling for couldn't speak a word of English. It was his simplicity which impressed me most. If there is love between two individuals, language is no barrier. We were soon married.'

Mr and Mrs Ali purchased a drapery shop selling clothes in Balsall Heath. Margaret ran the business whilst the back of the shop became a community centre. Zaman gave advice to newly arrived settlers from Pakistan and settled quarrels between husbands and wives. People came to him for guidance on their domestic or matrimonial problems. The people he helped called him *Chacha* or uncle to describe his caring and supportive ways.

Zaman became one of the prominent figures in the local Pakistani community and people looked to him for leadership. As the community grew in size, it sought the facilities that Muslim communities needed. Zaman led successful campaigns to establish an exclusive graveyard for Muslims and a slaughter

◑ *Choudhury Zaman Ali – the legendary Chacha of Birmingham.*

○ *Choudhury Zaman Ali's Scottish wife, Margaret (standing).*

house which upheld Islamic teaching on the killing of animals. He was also one of the men who secured the building of Birmingham's large Central Mosque in Highgate in the 1970s. Like other religious buildings in prominent sites in Birmingham, such as St Chad's Cathedral which served local Catholics and Singer's Hill Synagogue for the Jews, the Central Mosque demonstrated that local Muslims had established an important community in Birmingham.

Zaman's influence was not only local; he became one of the most important figures in the UK's Pakistani community when he served as President of the Muslim League in Britain. When prominent visitors came to this country from Pakistan, Zaman acted as their host. In his home village, he set up a school for girls and a hospital and provided ambulances for an area where they did not exist. The government of Pakistan awarded him the *Sitara-i-Khidmat* medal, which was like Britain's MBE, for his services to ordinary people.

Choudhury Zaman Ali died in 1983 at the age of eighty. People from all over the United Kingdom came to his funeral and the government of Pakistan also sent a representative to pay

⊕ *Choudhury Zaman Ali – A congregation in Birmingham.*

their respects. His work and example enabled many Pakistani migrants to adjust to life in Britain, but towards the end of his life he grew disillusioned with what he saw around him. He told the journalist Sultan Mahmood: 'Britain is not what she used to be. This country has seen many changes over the years. Violence, mugging, sexual freedom and an alarming increase in other crimes are all new things. There's a lot of racial hatred too. People do not like each other due to their different creed and colour of skin. They are also becoming less tolerant. I wonder where all those good English people have disappeared.'

Malcolm Dick

Reference

1. This biography was largely based on an article by Sultan Mahmood, "The legendary Chacha of Birmingham" *The Pakistani Times Overseas Weekly*, November 30, 1986.

The Memorial Gates Project: the Story of Altaf Hussain Chishti

The Memorial Gates Trust was set up with the aim of recognising the contribution made in both World Wars by the peoples of the Indian Sub-Continent, Africa and the Caribbean and providing a fitting memorial to their service. In 2002, the Memorial Gates were erected with the support of Millennium Commission Lottery funding across Constitution Hill at Hyde Park Corner, in London. Her Majesty the Queen opened the Memorial Gates on 6th November 2002.

Part of the commitment of the Memorial Gates Trust to the Millennium Commission was to produce an educational pack for schools. For some of the veterans interviewed for the educational materials, the lack of recognition for such service people was a source of distress. The Chair of the Memorial Gates Trust, Baroness Flather wrote: 'We would like to think that the next

⊕ *Alison Gove-Humphries with Altaf Hussain Chishti in Birmingham.*

41

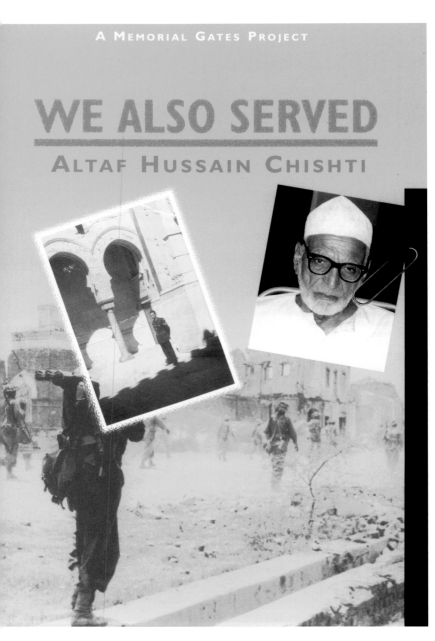

WE ALSO SERVED

ALTAF HUSSAIN CHISHTI

Memorial Gates Project's leaflet.

generation of British children, whether or not of ethnic minority origin, will not grow up without knowledge of such a massive contribution.' It was the purpose of the teaching pack 'We Also Served' – a pack of veterans' stories – to fulfil this aim. A team of reporters from community organisations and schools collected sixteen testimonies and personal accounts of Asian, African and African-Caribbean veterans who served in the First and Second World Wars.

I mentioned this project to a colleague of mine, Makhdoom Chishti, at a meeting of the Black Pasts, Birmingham Futures group. Makhdoom told me about his great grandfather who had helped the British during the First World War and his uncle, Altaf Hussain Chishti, who had served on the Allied side during World War II. We were looking for links between some of the service people and the Birmingham area. We agreed that Makhdoom should do the research and conduct an interview with his uncle and that I should write up the story. Makhdoom returned from Pakistan with a videoed interview with his uncle and a briefcase full of primary source materials relating to his great grandfather and uncle and their support for the British government. Then I wrote the story.

Altaf's family had a long history of supporting the British government. Altaf Hussain Chishti came from a village called Mangat, in what is now India. His grandfather – Fauj-ud-Din – was headman, or Zaildar, of 29 villages. He had helped to recruit soldiers during World War I. Altaf came from the Jat nation, a nation which was used to fighting. Altaf's cousin, Chaudery Abdul Hamid, took over as headman during World War II, thanks to Altaf writing a letter on his behalf to the British authorities. Chaudery Abdul Hamid also recruited soldiers for the British army.

Altaf himself was 17 in 1939 when World War II broke out and he got very excited when he saw the soldiers marching along the road near his school. He was 19 when he joined the

Supply Branch of the Royal Indian Army Service Corps on 24th April 1942. After several months of training, Altaf was sent to the Burma Front with 39 Division. They served in the area between Mandalay and Rangoon.

Three episodes stand out for me in the story of Altaf Hussain Chishti's wartime experience:

When he first reached Rangoon, Altaf can remember one evening when the soldiers were sitting around talking. It was full moonlight. Suddenly, the skies lit up with fire. The soldiers were so new to warfare that they thought someone was getting married and they were watching a firework show. The captain soon came out and told them it was enemy aircraft gun fire and ack-ack fire and he said to them, very calmly, 'Why don't you go into your trenches?'

There was a training session near Hardewar. Altaf was in one of two brigades training in jungle warfare. One brigade had to attack another but they were forbidden to use gunfire because it would show the 'enemy' where they were. It was night time and one of the soldiers, a sergeant, jumped into a trench. There was a lion sleeping there. A fight took place between the soldier and the lion and the soldier killed the lion with his bayonet (the knife on the end of his rifle). He had obviously stuck obediently to the rules and would not use his gun. When the soldiers returned to their camp, they wondered where the sergeant had gone. In the morning, they went looking for him and found him in the trench next to the lion – both dead.

There was a shortage of cigarettes, but one British soldier was smoking Woodbines and boasting about having these cigarettes. To the surprise of the Indian soldiers, his captain, who was standing nearby, slapped him on the cheek and said 'You idiot! Don't you know there's a shortage of cigarettes? You're smoking in front of Indian soldiers. What will they think? That we're enjoying ourselves and getting the best of everything and they're not.' Apparently, the British soldiers were given superior cigarettes to Indian soldiers who were given a make of cigarettes called 'Lamps'.

Altaf left the army in July 1947 and Pakistan was formed that year. He went on to fight in Kashmir from 1947-49. Altaf subsequently trained as a Flight Sergeant in the Pakistan Air Force. He now lives in Gullalipur in Pakistan.

Alison Gove-Humphries

11

Kurds

The Kurdish Community

The West Midlands is home to about four to five thousand Kurdish asylum seekers and refugees, the vast majority from Iraq. Kurdistan or Kurdland does not exist as a separate country; it is divided between several states. With their distinct language and culture, Kurds live in Iran, Iraq, Turkey, Syria and Russia. They form the largest nationality in the world that does not have its own homeland. After the defeat and collapse of the Turkish Ottoman Empire in the Middle East after World War I,

Britain together with France was largely responsible for the division of Turkish possessions and Kurds were denied self-government. Britain ruled Iraq until after World War II. For decades, the international community supported governments which suppressed the Kurds, including Saddam Hussein when he first came to power. Iraqi Kurdistan now forms part of a post-Saddam Iraq and its potential for self-determination and economic development is probably greater than at any time in recent history.

The first Kurdish refugees came in small numbers to Britain in 1958. In 1982 and 1991 numbers increased following uprisings, the aftermath of the First Gulf War and the brutal actions

◉ *This Sena Killim rug is a famous killim design from the West of Iran, Kurdistan. Sena is the old name of the city, where it originated. It is made with wool on cotton weaving.*

of Saddam Hussein's regime. Kurds survived Arab control of their oil resources, chemical warfare, which killed thousands of people, deportation from their homes, the denial of freedom and mass terror from the Iraqi government. Kurds were normally unable to seek safe havens in nearby countries, so many settled in Europe.

One of the refugees who came in 1982 was Sarwar Mohammad. Born into a political family his three brothers were killed and at the age of 12 he was imprisoned and tortured. His nose was broken and he was forced to witness the rape and torture of others. Close to death he was released from prison and was lucky to receive hospital treatment to save his life, but he remained scarred, physically and psychologically. Escaping to Iran, he was able to get a passport and fly to England. He was hospitalised almost immediately, but he was given refugee status in 15 days. His time in England was hard, facing poverty, exploitation from employers and the need to study to improve his situation. He spends much of his time helping other Kurdish refugees and people seeking asylum.

Most Kurdish people in the West Midlands are young men who escaped from Saddam Hussein's Iraq in the first years of the twenty-first century, but there are also families and Kurdish women in the community. Many are educated, highly skilled people who respect democracy and British traditions. They have lived with traumatic experiences which most British people can only imagine. As asylum seekers and refugees, many local Kurds face poverty, racism, poor housing, unscrupulous landlords, unemployment or employment in poorly paid occupations. One Kurdish job seeker was asked by a potential employer if he was a terrorist. The man and his family, in fact had been victims of Saddam Hussein's terrorism when their home town of Halabja was attacked by chemical weapons. Nevertheless, local Kurds have established self-help organisations to provide advice to members of the community on housing, health care, education, jobs and information about British life and civilisation. Others have entered the professions and created businesses. Critical to their survival has been determination and self-belief. As Sarwar Mohammed said, 'It does not matter who you are or where you are, if you believe in yourself you can do anything you want.'

Malcolm Dick

References

1. Dick, Malcolm, *Celebrating Sanctuary, Birmingham and the Refugee Experience 1750 – 2002* (Refugee Action, 2002).
2. Dick, Malcolm, Interviews with members of the Kurdish Community conducted in 2001 – 2004.
3. Regional Surveys of the World, *The Middle East and North Africa*, various editions, (London, various dates).

12

Somalis

The Somali Community

Somalis come from the Horn of Africa in the east of the continent. Both African and Arabic influences have shaped their cultural identity and Islam is the main religion. During their history, Somalis have been influenced by many foreign powers, including Egypt, Turkey, Italy, France and Britain. They have experienced a history of invasion, partition and occupation and, in recent years, Ethiopia and Kenya have annexed Somali territory. In the post-colonial period, creating a national identity has been hard. The Somali Republic dates from 1960, but political instability, military government, conflict with Ethiopia and civil war have devastated and divided the country. Many thousands of people are refugees in nearby countries and Europe and North America.

Britain's first contact with Somalis was in the early nineteenth century through the port of Berbera in the north of the country which was linked to trade and transport between Europe and India. In 1827 the British signed a treaty with Somalis in Berbera and that began the process of northern Somalia becoming a British colony.

Somalis are one of the oldest immigrant communities in the UK, and can be dated back to the nineteenth century. They started coming to the UK with British ships as sailors initially for a short stay. Visible numbers of early Somali communities started developing in the coastal cities of Cardiff, Liverpool, Hull, and London. Some of them worked in the busy docks and later in the steel industry in towns such as Sheffield. Somalis also worked with British forces in the Second World War and some ex-soldiers were offered work on Royal Naval mail after the war.

It was after the civil war in Somalia (1991 – 1995) that substantial numbers of the Somali community started coming to the UK, Europe and to other parts of the world as refugees fleeing conflict and hostility in their own country.

The Somali population in Birmingham is growing in number because many families choose to settle in the city. Some members of the community come from other parts of UK while others come from the countries of the European Union, such as Holland, Germany and Sweden. There are no official statistics about the Somali population in Birmingham but what is clear is that their number is growing rapidly. This is evidenced by the number of Somalis coming to the advice centres to access services and children waiting for school placements.

The last baseline study conducted in 2000 in Birmingham estimated the Somali population at less than 2,000 persons. Since then the population has exponentially increased with a conservative estimate putting the Somali population in Birmingham now around 4,500 people.

Somalis are Sunni Muslims and share the same language and culture. In Somali culture and tradition family cohesiveness is very strong in broad terms covering both the immediate family members and the extended ones. Some of the reasons Somalis are coming to Birmingham include friends, family ties and the large Muslim community in the city. However, the community is one of the most disadvantaged and most deprived. The Somali community has many unmet needs including poor housing and homelessness, unemployment and limited educational qualifications.

Language barriers, lack of knowledge of how British officialdom works, school underachievement and racism all increase the barriers which face this community.

The Somali community is business minded and entrepreneurial and that can be seen by the numbers of small business that have been created independently in a relatively short time. The community is also in the process of establishing self-help organisations, such as the East African Community Advice and Support Bureau in Sparkhill.

Mohammed Aden

◑ *18th Century Turkish embroidery [Courtesy of COL Cards].*

13

Yemenis

The Yemeni Community

The Yemeni community in Britain can be traced back to 1885. South Yemen was then part of the British Empire and Britain occupied the important port of Aden until 1967. The Yemen is a particularly significant Arab country. Its civilisation goes back thousands of years and in the ancient world it was a source of frankincense and myrrh and the legendary home of the Queen of Sheba. There is a unique architectural tradition and the version of Arabic spoken there is the closest to the classical language in which the Qur'ân was written. For many years the Yemen has exported labour and the first settlers in Britain were those who had served on British merchant ships or as soldiers

○ *Farhan Almaflahi (Yemeni) with Islamic calligraphy.*

in the British army. The most famous contemporary Yemeni in Britain is the boxer, Prince Naseem Hamid, from Sheffield. The Yemeni community in Birmingham has a substantial history.

The first Yemenis came to Birmingham in the early twentieth century to find work in the local metal trades. Industrious workers, many laboured in poor conditions and for low pay in factories where accidents and injuries were common. The growth in migration was significant in the 1950s and 1960s, but in the 1970s industrial decline led to unemployment and many left the UK. Most Yemenis arrived as single men and families followed later, if at all. There is still a significant population of elderly single men in the city who have lived locally for decades. It is difficult to estimate the size of the Yemeni population in Birmingham as census figures and other records do not provide this information.

○ *Al-Yafai for Orientals – Ladypool Road, Birmingham.*

A recent survey of the social and economic needs of the community in 1998, estimated that between 5,000 and 7,000 people of Yemeni origin lived in Birmingham, mainly in Small Heath, Balsall Heath, Sparkbrook, Highgate and Edgbaston.

The best-known local Yemeni is Shaikh Muhammad Qassim al'Alawi who died in Birmingham in 1999 at the age of ninety. As a boy he looked after sheep in the Yemeni village of Shamir, but in 1925, at the age of fifteen, he moved to Cardiff and joined the British merchant navy. After seeing the world he joined the Cardiff branch of the 'Alawl Sufi Order and dedicated the rest of his life to religion and public service. By the 1940s, Birmingham possessed a small Yemeni community and many men married local women. There were few opportunities for Yemenis to practise their religion and they lost contact with their Islamic roots. In 1941 Shaikh Muhammad moved to Balsall Heath where many Yemenis had their homes. He set up the city's first *zawiya* or centre for prayer and became the spiritual leader and guide of the community for nearly sixty years. The zawiya deserves to be recognised as Birmingham's first mosque. Shaikh Mohammad's significance spread beyond Birmingham. When he died the brother of the President of the Yemen attended his funeral.

Locally the community has several characteristics. Though Yemenis speak Arabic and belong to the Islamic Faith, there are divisions as many Yemenis see themselves as either from the south or the north of the country or members of particular tribal groups. This reflects different historical traditions and the bitter civil war, which affected the country from 1962 to 1970. These experiences are sources of identity for many Yemenis, but others express concern about the differences. In the Birmingham context, these divisions have prevented the community from providing a united representative organisation.

Despite the long-term presence of the Yemeni community, which predates mass migration from South Asia and the

○ *Ali Al-Yafai – A Yemeni.*

Caribbean in the 1950s and 1960s, it remained an invisible minority for decades. It was largely ignored by official organisations and suffered from multiple disadvantages. These included high levels of unemployment, lack of opportunities for women, poor access to education and advice, language difficulties, low quality housing, limited health education and a lack of support services for older people. Only recently has the City Council started to translate documents into Arabic. This in itself is not sufficient, as many Yemenis are illiterate in their own language. The Education Department now keeps statistics on the progress of Yemeni pupils. As a result, additional support, targeted specifically on teaching and supporting Yemenis is available.

Despite these problems, the community strengthened its profile in the 1990s. Individuals improved their educational qualifications and created small businesses in the retail sector. In many Yemeni households women have faced cultural restrictions, which limited access to education, employment and independence. The Yemeni Women's Association is one way in which a group of young women have organised themselves to raise their status and profile. The registered charity, Yemeni Elderly, in Small Heath and Sparkbrook, has been created to provide advice, support, befriending and advocacy services to a particularly vulnerable and disadvantaged group. Two other organisations have played a significant role in enhancing the political and cultural influence of the community, the Mu'ath Welfare Trust and the Yemeni Development Foundation.

Malcolm Dick

References

1. Dahya, Badr Ud-Din, 'South Asian Urban Immigration with Special Reference to Asian Muslim Immigrants in the English Midlands' (University of London, MSc Social Anthropology Thesis, 1967). The thesis concentrates on Yemeni migrants to Birmingham.

2. Dick, Malcolm, Interviews with members of the Yemeni Community, 2000 and 2001.

3. Halliday, Fred, *Arabs in Exile: Yemeni Migrants in Urban Britain* (I B Tauris, 1992). An excellent overview of the history of the Yemeni Community.

4. Muath Welfare Trust, *Amanah Newsletter*, various editions, 1999 – 2001.

5. Peter Dale Associates and The Steering Group of the Yemeni Community, *The Social and Economic Needs of the Yemeni Community in Birmingham* (Swindon, Peter Dale Associates, 2000).

6. Yemeni Development Foundation, *Annual Reports* and www.ydf.org.uk.

Aalaa al-Shamahi

Aalaa al-Shamahi, was born in Birmingham in 1983. Her parents came from the Yemen. Some ten years later she joined Young Muslims, a social organisation for Muslims from different cultures.

One interesting thing was that we had Muslims from so many different backgrounds. We had converts from the black communities and the white communities and so I actually became Pakistani in the way I did things and I think the Yemeni girls didn't like that at all 'You've just left your identity behind. What's the point of that?'

But as I got older within Young Muslims, I started to go back to my Arab roots for the sake of Arabic (the language) and also because I have a love affair with the desert. I just really love the desert…some things I can't explain, it's just this love that you have in your heart and it's very difficult to explain because I have the same love for England. There are some things within England that I just can't bear to live without. Because of that I classified myself as a Muslim because that is the only thing that I could fully agree with. From everything else I took bits and I left bits and I didn't regard that as my full identity.

Reference

1. This extract from the transcript of an oral history interview with Aalaa al-Shamahi was conducted by Helen Lloyd for the Millennibrum Project in 2001, Birmingham City Archives, MS 2255/144. A copy of the original minidisk recording and transcript are available for consultation in Local Studies and History, Floor 6 of Birmingham Central Library.

Birmingham Mosques

A mosque is a place of worship where Muslims gather for prayer. It also serves as a social and cultural centre for local communities. The first mosque in Birmingham was established and financed by two Yemeni Muslims in 1941 in Edward Road, Balsall Heath. Before the 1970s mosques were generally created without registering with local authorities as places of worship. When planning permission was sought, the City Council showed reluctance to grant permission, imposing restrictions and conditions that were difficult to meet. Some of the coverage in newspapers reflected local hostility to other cultures in general and Islam in particular.

As a result of a campaign of persuasion by, amongst others, Jalal Uddin, the representative for Islam on the Birmingham Council of Faiths, it has been easier to obtain permission. By 1987 there were 55 mosques in Birmingham and by 2005 there were over 80. Many of these are small and located in private homes. Others are former public buildings, including a number of distinguished Victorian schools, which have outlived their original purposes and been given new leases of life as places of worship. Some new mosques are elaborate purpose-built complexes containing prayer-halls, libraries, schoolrooms and even marriage bureaux.

A number of purpose-built mosques have become significant features of the local landscape. The Central Mosque in Highgate, on a prominent hilltop position, is one significant local feature. It was completed in 1975 and contains a large prayer hall with space for 3,000 worshippers. The building provides a place of worship for people of African, African Caribbean, Asian and white European origin. The Darul Uloom Islamia Mosque, in Small Heath, was the biggest in Europe when it was built in the 1980s. It could accommodate 5,000 worshippers. Its creation

⊙ *Islamia Aladuia Zawiya – Edward Road, Balsall Heath, Birmingham.*

was a considerable achievement for the community, which raised the £2.3 million pounds to finance construction. Volunteers did a lot of the building work, and this kept costs down. The growth in the number of mosques is testimony to the thriving nature of Islam in Birmingham, one of the most important centres for the religion in Europe.

Most mosques developed to serve people from a particular geographical area and cultural group, for example Punjabi, Mirpuri (Azad Kashmiri), Bangladeshi and Yemeni Muslims. The Imams lead the prayers, deliver sermons and provide coun-

⊙ *Birmingham Central Mosque – Belgrave Middleway, Highgate, Birmingham.*

selling and advice. They are scholars who have been trained in religious studies and Islamic law. Traditionally most Imams in Birmingham came from abroad, but by the late 1980s about a quarter were recruited locally. To serve a need the Darul Uloom Islamia Mosque founded a college to train local Imams.

Mosques also serve as community centres, managed by a chairman and employing administrators. Inside children learn the Qur'ân and attend classes teaching the language of their country of origin. Larger mosques serve as centres for advice and welfare and provide sports facilities, a bookshop and a library.

Malcolm Dick

References

1. Dick, Malcolm, Interviews with local Muslims, including Jalal Uddin, 2000 and 2001.
2. Gale, Richard, 'The multicultural city and the politics of religious architecture: urban planning, mosques and meaning-making in Birmingham, UK', *Built Environment*, *30*(1), 2004.
3. Joly, Daniele, *Britannia's Crescent: making a Place for Muslims in British Society* (Aldershot, 1995).

⬆ *Central Jamia Mosque 'Ghamkolvia' – Golden Hillock Road, Small Heath, Birmingham.*

The Jamiah Masjid (Main Mosque), Handsworth, Birmingham

The Birchfield Road Flyover in Perry Barr speeds the traveller past the Jamiah Masjid or Main Mosque. Originally named after President Saddam Hussein, this redbrick building with its golden dome, stained-glass windows and spacious interiors, provides an elegant contrast to the tower blocks and terraced homes which dominate this part of Birmingham. In 1988, President Saddam Hussein of Iraq donated the sum of £2 million for the construction of this Sunni mosque. Not surprisingly, it was named after its financial patron. Then Saddam was Britain's friend. He had launched a war against Iran, a Shi'a Muslim state that was hostile to western influence in the Middle East. Much of Saddam's weaponry was manufactured locally. Many of his tanks began life in Coventry and the 'Iraqi supergun' was built in Halesowen. According to a senior member of the mosque, 'Saddam was Britain's best friend then. He was fighting Iran and keeping half of the West Midlands in work!'

Saddam became an enemy of Britain and the USA following his invasion of Kuwait in 1991. The United Nations backed the First Gulf War in 1991 to repel the invasion and Saddam became a figure of hate in Britain. The mosque was attacked and fire bombing caused several thousand pounds worth of damage. The building remained vulnerable, but served as a major community centre within an increasingly diverse Islamic community in Aston and Handsworth. The

➊ *The Jamiah Masjid (Main Mosque) previously known as Saddam Hussein Mosque, Birchfield Road, Handsworth, Birmingham.*

first worshippers were Gujarati Muslims, Pakistanis and Bangladeshis, but the coming of refugees to Handsworth, led to a more varied membership containing Bosnians, Kurds and Somalis, including people fleeing from Saddam's Iraq.

During the Second Gulf War in 2003, the elders of the mosque decided to change the name of their place of worship. The President Saddam Hussein Mosque was reborn as the Jamiah Masjid (Main Mosque), a common name for many Muslim places of worship. The building remains as a striking architectural feature of Birmingham's skyline, but its distinctiveness is now disguised by its low-profile label.

Malcolm Dick

References

1. The main sources for this article were secured via a web search for Saddam Hussein Mosque Birmingham. An earlier version of the article appears on the Digital Handsworth website: www.digitalhandsworth.org.uk.

Islamic Relief

Islamic Relief was founded in 1984 at a time of terrible famine in Ethiopia and the Sudan by Dr Hany El-Banna and other students at the University of Birmingham. Originally known as Help Muslim Refugees in Africa, the name was changed as a result of a suggestion from Yusuf Islam, formerly known as Cat Stevens, the pop singer and convert to Islam. He proposed the snappier title, Islamic Relief. It became an international relief and development organisation with a multi-million pound programme sponsoring projects in over 22 countries by the year 2000. Supported by the British Government and the United Nations, Islamic Relief has its headquarters in Birmingham and offices throughout the world.

Islamic Relief faced many challenges in the 1990s, floods in Bangladesh, famine in the Sudan, and earthquakes in Iran and Armenia, but the organisation showed an ability to respond swiftly to events. During the Gulf War, Richard Branson took a plane to Jordan with goods from England to help refugees who had arrived from Kuwait or Iraq. 40 tons of the aid material was from Islamic Relief. Linda Chalker the Overseas Development Minister went to the refugee camps and helped to distribute materials to the refugees. These landmarks helped Islamic Relief to raise awareness of its work within British society.

In its early years, Islamic Relief concentrated on fund raising and emergency relief, but its work extended to include rehabilitation and development projects as well as responding to immediate crises. Islamic Relief has provided emergency aid after earthquakes in Iran, cyclones in Bangladesh and India and food and accommodation for people displaced by conflict in Chechnya. In Bosnia local people were helped to start farms and refugees in Kosovo have been resettled. Major long-term projects have included providing clean water, sanitation, health, education and small business development throughout many countries in Africa, Asia and Europe.

Islamic Relief does not confine its work to Muslims. Most of its money comes from Muslim donors, a response to the Islamic principle of Zakah, the duty to provide for the poor and needy, but it has co-operated with Oxfam, Cafod (Catholic Aid for Overseas Development) and other Christian agencies in different parts of the world including Ethiopia and El Salvador. In 2001 an earthquake hit the Gujarat in India and Islamic Relief sent an emergency team to distribute food and tents. Christian Aid did not have a programme there and it donated to Islamic Relief to assist the relief programme for Christians, Hindus and Sikhs in the area. According to Dr Hany El-Banna: 'Our strategy comes

↻ *Dr. Hany El-Banna – founder of Islamic Relief.*

from the Hadith (the tradition of the prophet Muhammed, peace be upon him), that every living soul deserves charity. I do not differentiate; I do not segregate people because of their colour, their race, or their religion or their background…the merciful man cannot differentiate between races at the time of disaster.'

During a visit to Islamic Relief, Clare Short, the Birmingham MP and former Minister for International Development described the organisation as a 'centre of goodness' combating violence, distress and intolerance across the world.

Although Islamic Relief is the best-known of all local Muslim relief organisations, it is one of several charitable organisations which reflect Islamic teaching on Zakah or almsgiving.

Malcolm Dick

References

1. Islamic Relief, Miscellaneous printed and video material in the possession of the author.
2. Much information is taken from the transcript of an oral history interview with Dr Hany El-Banna, which was conducted by Lorraine Blakemore for the Millennibrum Project in 2001, Birmingham City Archives (Ref: MS 2255/149). A copy of the original minidisk recording and transcript are available for consultation in Local Studies and History, Floor 6 of Birmingham Central Library.
3. www.islamic-relief.org.uk.

Victoria Square, Birmingham City Centre, which receives its name from the statue of Queen Victoria, unveiled on 10th January 1901 (just before her death). As well as statues and memorials the City Centre contains many of Birmingham's heritage buildings and attractions. The Council House is situated opposite a massive water feature. It is the largest fountain in Europe with a flow of 3,000 gallons per minute, representing life force and youth. The City Centre holds regular multi-cultural events. A regular feature between November and December is the Frankfurt Christmas Market, held in Victoria Square and New Street, where over 50 stalls offer Christmas gifts and a range of unusual gift ideas.

Image Gallery 1

Celebrations and Cultures

Celebrations and Festivals

⬆ *Muslim worshippers are gathering for Eid prayer.*
➡ *Muslim worshippers offering the Eid prayer.*

🔼 *Dr. Muhammad Naseem having a dialogue with a Muslim fellow brother.*
➡️ *A Muslim worshipper with his son.*
🔽 *Muslim worshippers at the front of the Birmingham Central Mosque.*

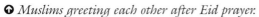
⬆ *Muslims greeting each other after Eid prayer.*
➡ *Volunteers are counting the collection for the Mosque on Eid day.*
⬇ *Muhammad Akber Khan (left) with his friends, after Eid prayer.*

⬆ *Cricketer Mushtaq Muhammad greeted by a Muslim fellow brother.*

⬇ *Members of diverse Muslim communities at the front yard of Birmingham Central Mosque after the Eid prayer.*

61

⬆ *Muhammad Najeeb (left), Choudhry Muhammad Afzal and the late Dost Muhammad Khan at Birmingham Central Mosque, Highgate, Birmingham on Eid day.*

⬅ *M Saad Bhatti (left), PC Anthony Fischer shaking hands with M Imtiaz Bhatti after Eid prayer.*

⬇ *Muhammad Ali with his Children, Muazzam Ali (left) and Shahmir Ali.*

Fabrics and Dresses

⬆ *Hand made embroidered Kashmiri wool shawl for females.*

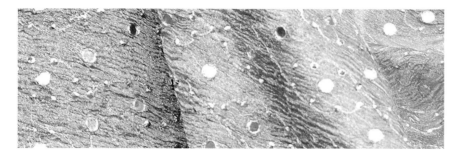

⬆ *Crinkle tissue and organza textiles for women's suits.*

⬆ *Embroidery (called Veera Zaara) on Crepe.*
➡ *A Jat girl wearing a beautiful embroidered Kashmiri shawl.*

⬆ *Hand made pashmina shawl with silk embroidery and mirrors.*
◀ *A Jat girl wearing a pashmina shawl.*
⬇ *Chiffon, crinkle and georgette fabrics for female dresses.*

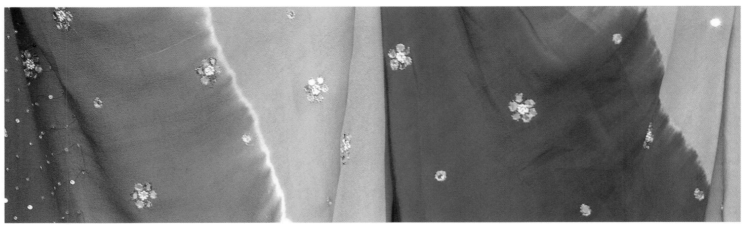

⬆ *Fishtail lahnga made from silk material – mixture of East and West design. A popular style of dress for young Muslim girls.*

⬆ *Turban usually called a Kullah – distinguished gentlemen wear these in the community, as a mark of honour. Dr. Ghulam Murtaza reciting Saiful Muluk at White Pearl, Birmingham on Pakistan Independence celebration.*

Wedding Ceremony

⬆ *Bride with her younger brother.*
⬅ *Bride arriving at menhdi (henna) ceremony.*
⬇ *Menhdi ceremony.*

↑ *Groom arriving at a wedding ceremony being welcomed by the bride's grandmother.*

➲ *Bride with her cousins.*

↓ *Doli – a sedan, formerly used for a bride to travel from her parents' home to the groom's house.*

● *Groom.*
● *Bride.*

Food and Food Preparation

⬆ *Lahore Sweet shop at Ladypool Road, Balsall Heath, Birmingham.*

⬅ *Arabic sweets.*

➡ *Kulfi – Asian ice cream.*

⬋ *Naseer Khan holding prepared Chicken tikka, Lahore Kebab House at Ladypool Road, Birmingham.*

⬊ *Nafees Ahmad in the process of preparing chicken tikka on naan.*

↑ *Chef, Shah Alam Khan, preparing a naan.*

↗ *Chef taking out the naan from the tandoor (oven).*

← *Chef making sheesh kebab – the name is traced to the Turkish Sheesh Kebab, which means a spicy morsel of meat grilled on a skewer.*

→ *Chef Nafees Ahmad, with sheesh kebabs on skewers.*

↘ *Sheesh kebabs being charcoal grilled.*

Section B
Windows on Islam

Windows on Islam: Introduction

This section of the publication defines the basic practices of Islam and what is expected of a true Muslim. The chapters in this section look initially at the five pillars of Islam:

- ▶ Faith (Shahadah)
- ▶ Prayer (Salat)
- ▶ Fasting in Ramadan (Siyam)
- ▶ Almsgiving (Zakah)
- ▶ Pilgrimage to Makkah (Hajj)

These duties are illustrated by looking at how five individuals in the West Midlands have interpreted them in their personal lives. Four of the five statements are taken from the transcripts of oral histories conducted by the Millennibrum Project in 2000 and 2001. This was a multi-media community history project in Birmingham which created a range of materials to illustrate patterns of life and living in the city after 1945.

Other pieces in *Windows on Islam* offer perspectives on the Islamic Year and Festivals, Muslim Life and Women's Rights and Responsibilities.

Verdah Chishti

⬆ *Discover Islam, The Reader [Source: Trabscin International (USA) and Taibah International Aid Association, 1997].*

Faith (Shahadah)

Muslims believe that the revelations of Islam came from Allah (God) to the Prophet Muhammad 🕌 (Peace Be Upon Him) via the Angel Jibra'il (Gabriel). However, the faith did not begin from the Prophet Muhammad 🕌 (PBUH) but was renewed and completed by him. The faith actually began with Abraham, Moses and Jesus. For Muslims, the Qur'ân is the direct word of Allah, delivered to the Prophet Muhammad 🕌 (PBUH) between 610 and 632 AD in the city of Makkah (Mecca).

Every religion in the world has a meaningful name. Islam is an Arabic word which means submission, surrender and obedience. As a religion, Islam stands for complete submission and obedience to Allah. A person, who freely and consciously accepts the Islamic way of life and holds and practices the three fundamental beliefs of the religion, is called a Muslim. The three fundamental Islamic beliefs are:

- Tawhid (oneness of Allah)
- Risalah (prophethood)
- Akhirah (life after death)

The most fundamental belief in Islam is faith in the unity of Allah, which is expressed in the Primary Kalima or phrase:

'La Ilaha Illallah Muhammad Ur Rasool Allah' in Arabic, which means, in English: 'There is no God but Allah and Muhammad 🕌 (Peace Be Upon Him) is the Prophet of Allah'. The Kalima has been translated into various languages to reflect on the diversity of the Muslim community, as can be seen over the page:

Two Muslims offer reflections on their belief. The first, Sultan Mahmood, came to England from Pakistan in 1960 and the second, Abdul Ahmed, who was born on the Caribbean island of Nevis and converted to Islam in 1994, describe what their faith means to them.

Aasma Nazir

⊙ *Islamic Calligraphy.*

আল্লাহ্ ছাড়া আর কোন মাবুদ নেই, এবং
মোহাম্মদ (সাঃ আঃ) আল্লাহর প্রেরীত রাসূল।

Bengali

ਅੱਲਾ ਤੋਂ ਬਿਨਾ ਹੋਰ ਕੋਈ ਰੱਬ ਨਹੀਂ ਅਤੇ ਮੁਹੰਮਦ (ਰੱਬ ਉਸ ਨੂੰ
ਸ਼ਾਂਤੀ ਦੇਵੇ) ਅੱਲਾ ਦਾ ਰਸੂਲ ਹੈ।

Punjabi

Nema drugog Boga do Alaha, a Muhamed
[Mir neka bude s njim] je njegov prorok

Bosnian

نشته هیڅ معبود مگر د الله (ﺭ) ﯕﺨﻪ او محمد ﷺ د اللّه(ﺭ) پیغمبر دی

Pushto

نیست هیچ معبودی مگر الله (ﺝ) و محمد (ﺹ) و پیامبر الله (ﺝ)
است

Farsi

**Нет Б-га кроме Аллаха, и Мохамед
[и мир его над ним] пророк Аллаха.**

Russian

अल्लाह के अतिरिक्त कोई माबूद नहीं, और मोहम्द (माबूद उसे शांति दे)
अल्लाह का पैगम्बर है।

Hindi

ILaahay mooyee alle kale ma jiro, Muxamadna [Nabadgalyo
iyo Naxariis korkiisa ha ahaatee] waa rasuulkii ILaahay.

Somali

هیچ خودایەك نییه تەنھا الله نەبن، وه موحەمەد
[درودی خوای لێ بن] پێغەمبەری ئەوه.

Kurdish

اللہ کے سوا کوئی معبود نہیں اور محمّد اللہ کے رسُول ہیں

Urdu

A Reflection on Faith by Sultan Mahmood

All religions tell you the same thing: don't hurt other people, don't upset other people, respect other people, don't commit crimes. What's happening unfortunately these days in the Middle East is just not Islam. I am a Muslim and my religion is called Islam. Islam means peace. Our holy prophet Muhammad 	(PBUH) used to entertain Jews in the Mosque. It is a totally wrong concept that Islam was spread with the sword.

In Islamic ideology, in Zakah, rich people are supposed to give so much every week, every month and the poor people of the society are looked after. Now this is what the Social Security system is all about. Islam tells us not to tell lies, not to cheat, not to deceive other people. Islam is not only to offer your prayers five times but also to try to avoid committing sins. That's what Islam is all about and I think these are the things which Christianity professes also.

Being a good Muslim, you are not supposed to do something which is offensive to other people. Islam totally and utterly rejects militancy. You can't conquer the hearts of the people by force. You conquer the hearts of the people by arguments, by dialogue, by extending the hand of friendship.

As I've become older I realise how much I've begun to bond with Allah and how much I feel I need him and have advanced because of my belief in Him. Sometimes I have to thank Him and sometimes I have to ask for stuff. I read the Qur'ân every day. It's increased over time; it's something that I feel is part of me.

A Reflection on Faith by Abdul Ahmed

I don't drink, I don't take drugs and I am definitely not crazy, but I had a vision of myself as a Muslim and it is that that instantly told me who I was. When I first started going to the mosque, I used to sneak a look along the line at everybody's feet and I couldn't see any difference between my feet and theirs. In terms of colour all feet seemed the same. However, there were Africans there, there were African-Caribbeans there, there were Bangladeshis and people from Pakistan, there were English people there, there were Irish people there, all along this line and all the feet were the same. I couldn't see one foot that was darker than the other. And I used to smile it was just so right....

I never felt out, different or removed from them although there is all these different languages going on around me. I never felt left out because I couldn't understand what they were saying, I knew what it meant...that you are the one, there is one god, you are all his children and he loves you all and you need to love him – end of story really.

There is a growing trend amongst African Caribbean males to convert to Islam and the reasons I am sure are numerous. Personally, I don't care what the reasons are, as long as they do and that is not to say that Islam is a superior religion to any other religion. I just believe that there is a need for human beings to acknowledge that there is a Creator, that there is a God. Whether you want to call it Christianity, Hinduism, Sikhism or whatever, I don't think it matters much as long as you believe in something beyond ourselves; at the end of the day that is probably what saves us from destroying this beautiful world that we live in.

References

1. 	 This is an Arabic script which is used after Muhammad. It's meaning is Peace Be Upon Him.
2. These extracts from transcripts of oral history interviews with Sultan Mahmood and Abdul Ahmed were conducted by Helen Lloyd for the Millennibrum Project in 2001, Birmingham City Archives (Refs MS 2255/072 and MS 2255/013). Copies of the original minidisk recordings and transcripts are available for consultation in Local Studies and History, Floor 6 of Birmingham Central Library.

⬆ *Islamic calligraphy exhibited on Eid Milan Meena Bazaar 2001, Symphony Hall, Birmingham.*

Prayer (Salat)

● *A Muslim
artist's expression
about prayer.*
● *Prayer mat.*

Muslims are required to offer Salat five times at specific times during the day. Times are fixed in relation to the position of the sun. During Salat, Muslims face towards the Káaba (House of Allah) in Makkah. The Prophet Ibrāhīm (Abraham), (Peace Be Upon Him), the patriarch of Jews, Christians, and Muslims rebuilt the Káaba, as the focal point for the worship of Allah. The prayer should be followed by ritual washing and cleansing.

Aasma Nazir

Learning to Pray

Shahista Zamir was born in Glasgow in 1982. Her parents were Pakistani and subsequently divorced. From the age of eight, Shahista moved to Birmingham to live with her mother and stepfather. She describes how prayer became important in her life.

I started going to the mosque when I was twelve years old which was in 1995. My education in Scotland was quite limited before my mum and dad got divorced. As a Muslim child I should have finished the Qur'ân before I was about 10 or 11 because everyone expects that. When I did come back here, I was quite unsatisfied that I didn't have this Arabic education that I should have received as a Muslim and I spoke to my step father and he was very happy to take me down to the Central Mosque in Birmingham. I learned how to pray. I learned how to read the Qur'ân in Arabic even though I may not necessarily understand it. I was going to start a course where basically you learn to understand it, like you learn the literal translation of classic Arabic texts, but because my SATS were coming up I chose not to do that just yet.

Shahista Zamir

Reference

1. This extract from the transcript of an oral history interview with Shahista Zamir was conducted by Helen Lloyd for the Millennibrum Project in 2001, Birmingham City Archives, (Ref: MS 2255/145). A copy of the original minidisk recording and transcript are available for consultation in Local Studies and History, Floor 6 of Birmingham Central Library.

◉ *Children are taught the Qur'ân and prayer by an Imam at Madrasah in Birmingham (photographed by Nick Hedges).*

⬆ *Muslims in Birmingham performing their Friday prayer at Birmingham Central Mosque, Highgate, Birmingham.*
⬅ *Islamic Calligraphy.*

Fasting (Siyâm) in Ramadan

Muslims have to fast during the holy month of Ramadan, the ninth month of the Muslim calendar (Lunar) year. During fasting, from dawn to sunset one should not eat a grain of food nor drink a drop of water. The aim is to build up moral and spiritual values as well as increasing self-discipline, patience and selflessness.

Aasma Nazir

⊕ *Young Muslim girls reciting a fasting poem written by Abrar Din at the Eid and Christmas joint celebrations.*

Fasting

Abrar Din was 11 years old and a pupil at Wheelers Lane Technology College when he wrote this poem. It was published in a collection of poems produced in conjunction with Birmingham City Council's Millennibrum Project.

Wake up, wake up, Adnan said,
It's time to eat.
Yawning and eating
eating and yawning,
dark outside.
Time is running and dawn is breaking,
eyes are closing
can't seem to be opening,
still forcing myself to eat.
Dawn has broken,
no more eating or drinking until sunset.
My mouth is dry,
But can't drink any water.
Oh I wish it was time to open my fast.
It's been a long day
but I'll do it again tomorrow.

Abrar Din

Reference

1. *Peggy Nice and Trampy Man. School Words Three: Birmingham, a City of Poems*, Birmingham City Council, 2001.

Eid Al-Fitr

Eid Al-Fitr is celebrated once a year on the 1st Shawwal (10th lunar month). The month of Shawwal starts after the end of fasting – that is why it is called the festival of the breaking of the fast. Fasting which is undertaken on the month of Ramadan is one of the five pillars of Islam. Fitar comes from the word fatar meaning 'breaking'. Certain Sunni Muslims believe that Fitar comes from fitrat meaning 'nature'. Prior to this Eid, people fast for 29 or 30 days depending on the visibility of the moon for which Allah gives them the celebration of Eid as a present. In short, celebrating the first day of the new moon in Shawwal, marks the successful and peaceful end of Ramadan.

In the morning everyone bathes, wears new clothes and applies perfume. Women put mehndi (henna) on their hands on Eid Eve which is known as Chaand Raat (Moon Night). Each year this happens in Ladypool Road and Alum Rock Road in Birmingham as well as Southall (London) where females shop late at night and have henna painted on their hands. Special clothes with beautiful embroidery and designs are bought from these places and worn on the Eid day. Girls spend a lot of money on clothes, bangles, jewellery and shoes. Mostly, men wear the white shalwar kameez because it symbolises purity and austerity.

Early in the morning women prepare 'Sheer-khurma' or swaiyaan (noodles) cooked in sweetened milk and eat it as sunnah before going for Eid prayer. This dish is very popular and is the speciality of this Eid. People visit their relatives and friends graves, perhaps to honour their ancestors and to be with their spirits. On this festival people exchange Eid cards with their friends and relatives to share happiness among themselves and make visits to each others houses. Giving Eid presents and Eid money is another special part to show affection for others.

On Eid day everyone performs two Rakat Salat in the Jamiah (Central) mosque. These prayers can be read any time between sunrise and before afternoon. Men go to pray at Eid-Gha, in a big ground or Mosque whereas women prefer to pray at home. Eid milans (meetings) are part of the rituals in which people embrace each other three times, as is laid down in the Qur'ân.

Muslims are especially reminded of their obligations towards the poorer section of the society. A special contribution called 'Sadaqat-ul-Fiter' or 'Fitrana' is fixed for this purpose. This is paid by the head of the family on behalf of all the members of the family. It is compulsory to pay this before the Eid prayer so that poor people are able to join in the celebrations of the festival of the day. To a devout Muslim, Eid is a time to forget all past grievances and to spread love and harmony.

Farhana Tahir

🠕 *Eid Mubarak greetings card.*
🠔 *Each year a special feature on Eid is published by the Daily Jang, London. [Source: Courtesy of Daily Jang, London.]*

Almsgiving (Zakah)

Zakah is an obligatory payment by Muslims for charitable purposes. The amount is based on a rate of 2.5% of their annual savings. The money is to be spent on helping the poor and other welfare purposes. Zakah is not only given to individuals but is also provided to charity organisations for distribution.

Aasma Nazir

The Origins of Islamic Relief

Dr Hany El-Banna, an Egyptian Muslim who studied medicine at the University of Birmingham, created the charity Islamic Relief.

At the end of 1983 there was a big famine in Africa …remember the story of Bob Geldof and Band Aid and Live Aid? I was invited to attend a medical conference in the Sudan….After the conference somebody took me around to show me some of the refugee camps…it hit me so hard to see these kind of refugees, it actually became a challenge to do something for them. On the way back to England I stopped in Cairo and talked to my family about my visit to Sudan, and I started to earn some money to help the people in Sudan at the time. Then I went back to England, this was actually January 1984.

I sat down with one of my colleagues at Birmingham University to discuss what to do for Africa and we decided to open a bank account. We called it Help Moslem Refugees in Africa, and we banked the money which I raised in Cairo. Then I went to Birmingham University Islamic Society. On one of the Fridays I raised £300.00. I then asked Aston University Islamic Society. Again I raised about £250.00. My wife, my friend's wife, myself and my friend Dr Essan worked at home preparing the letters, appeals and all these sort of things.

We bought a small donation box and we put it in 517 Moseley Road, which still exists as the old address of Islamic Relief before it became Islamic Relief. We used to go there every Saturday to open the donation box and see how much was there, maybe a cheque for £5.00, a cheque for £20.00, a cheque for this and that, and people started to know us. They used to call us to give talks – Newcastle and Glasgow, Bradford, Leicester, London – about Africa at the time. When I used to raise £200.00 at the time, I was so happy to have this money. Some of the girls used to give their jewels. One of the most memorable donations which we received in August 1984 was £1,000.00. This was the biggest ever donation, I received since it was started in January….We stood up and we hugged one another, very proud of raising £1,000.00 from one individual, because £1,000.00 was for us a dream, and we were feeling that with this £1,000.00, we would be able to sort all the problems in Africa, and you can imagine how childish we were at the time.

Hany El-Banna

Reference

1. This extract from the transcript of an oral history interview with Dr Hany El Banna, was conducted by Lorraine Blakemore for the Millennibrum Project in 2001, Birmingham City Archives (Ref: MS 2255/149). A copy of the original minidisk recording and transcript are available for consultation in Local Studies and History, Floor 6 of Birmingham Central Library.

Pilgrimage to Makkah (Hajj)

The Hajj is the *Pilgrimage to Makkah* in *Islam*. It is the fifth of the *Five Pillars* in *Islam*.

The Hajj rituals have a deep psychological significance for Muslims. The pilgrimage is usually a very profound experience for those who participate in it. When life is lived according to

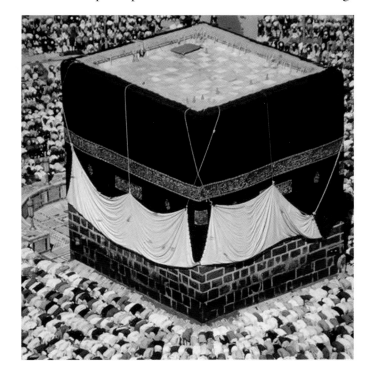

↑ *Káaba in Makkah, Saudi Arabia*
[Source: www.lexicorient.com/e.o/hajj.htm].

the precepts of the religion and the mind is in a suitable condition, the pilgrimage can spiritually transform the individual.

Hajj and its rites were first ordained by Allah in the time of the Prophet lbrahim (PBUH) [Abraham] and he was the one who was entrusted by Allah to build the Káaba – the House of Allah – along with his son Ishmāîl (PBUH) [Ishmael] at Makkah.

Allah described the Káaba and its building: 'And remember when We showed Ibrāhīm the site of the [Sacred] House [saying]: Associate not anything [in worship] with Me and purify My House for those who circumambulate it [perform tawaaf] and those who stand up for prayer and those who bow down and make prostration [in prayer etc.].' [*Surah Al-Hajj* 22:26]

The Hajj is the annual pilgrimage to Makkah which corresponds to Prophets Ibrāhīm (PBUH) [Abraham] and his son's series of sacred rites, these include wearing a special garment that symbolizes unity and modesty, collective circumambulations of the Káaba, the symbolic stoning of evil, sacrifices of animals and the holy festival Eid Al-Adha. Hajj is a religious obligation to be fulfilled at least once in the course of the life of each Muslim, who is physically and financially able to perform it. Literally, the word 'Hajj' means heading for an

↑ *Islamic Calligraphy.*

honourable place and legally it means worshipping Allah by performing the Hajj rituals, which are defined as specific acts performed at a specific time and place in a specific way. Hajj is performed on 9th Dhu Al-Hijjah in the twelfth month of the Islamic calendar.

It is a five-day series of rituals. Everyone wears two pieces of white cloth (Ihram) during the Hajj, which reinforces the concept of equality. The rites of the Hajj include circling the Káaba seven times and going seven times between the hillocks of Safa and Marwa, as Hagera, the mother of the Prophet Ismail did, during her search for water. Then the pilgrims stand together in Arafat, situated about 15 miles from Makkah, and ask Allah for what they wish and for His forgiveness, in what is often thought of as a preview of the Day of Judgement. The end of the Hajj is marked by a festival, Eid Al-Adha, which is celebrated with prayers.

The Káaba is situated at Haram mosque in Makkah. All Muslims face towards the Káaba when praying. The Káaba is the place of worship, which Allah commanded the Prophets Ibrāhīm (PBUH) [Abraham] and his son, to build.

The person who performs Hajj is called a 'Hajji'. Every year approximately 20,000 British citizens take part in this gathering of humanity. The following verses are recited frequently by the Hajji's during the Hajj.

لَبَّيْكَ اللّٰهُمَّ لَبَّيْكَ ، لَبَّيْكَ لَا شَرِيْكَ لَكَ لَبَّيْكَ
إِنَّ الْحَمْدَ وَ النِّعْمَةَ لَكَ وَ الْمُلْكَ لَا شَرِيْكَ لَكَ ،

'Labbaik Allahumma Labbaik. Labbaika, La Shareek Laka, Labbaik. Innal Hamdah, Wan Nematah, Laka wal Mulk, La Shareek Laka'

'Here I am at Thy service O Lord, here I am. Here I am at Thy service and Thou hast no partners. Thine alone is All Praise and All Bounty, and Thine alone is The Sovereignty. Thou hast no partners.'

Aasma Nazir

◗ *Islamic calligraphy.*

Eid Al-Adha

Eid Al-Adha is a three-day religious event and is one of the most important festivals of the Muslims. It is called Eid Al-Adha in Arabic and Bakr-Eid in Urdu. It is an occasion to give and to sacrifice. This festival is celebrated from 10th – 12th Dhul Hijja and marks the close of the Hajj or pilgrimage to the Káaba in Makkah. The history of this is related to the Prophet's willingness to sacrifice his son, on Allah's order. According to Islam, to test Ibrāhīm (PBUH) [Abraham], Allah commanded him, through a dream, to sacrifice his son. He agreed to do it but found himself unable to do this due to his paternal feelings, so he blindfolded himself before putting his son on the altar at the mount of Mina near Makkah. When he removed his blindfold, he saw his son standing alive in front of him and found a lamb instead of Ishmāîl (PBUH) [Ishmael].

On Eid Al-Adha, every Muslim must have a bath, wear new clothes, apply itar (perfume) and go to the mosque before eating anything, and recite the Takbir during their journey to mosque aloud in the following Arabic words:

اَللّٰهُ اَكْبَرُ اللّٰهُ اَكْبَرُ
لَا اِلٰهَ اِلَّا اَللّٰهُ
وَاللّٰهُ اَكْبَرُ اَللّٰهُ اَكْبَرُ
وَلِلّٰهِ الْحَمْدُ

Allah ho Akbar, Allah ho Akbar
La illaha illa Allah
Wa Allah ho Akbar, Allah ho Akbar
Wa Lillah hil Hamad

Allah is the greatest, Allah is the greatest
There is none worthy of worship except Allah
and Allah is the greatest, Allah is the greatest
and All praise for Allah

Everyone offers prayer (two Rakat Salat) in a Jamiah (central) mosque, which can be performed any time from sunrise to before afternoon. The prayer is more rewarding than daily or weekly offerings. Every Muslim who has wealth equal or more than 400 grams of gold is expected to sacrifice a goat, sheep or any four-legged animal (lamb, cow or camel), which is slaughtered during one of the three days of this festival and its meat is distributed. This meat should be divided into three equal parts: one part is for self, the second is for relatives and friends and the third part is for the poor and needy.

This festival is celebrated for three days. People wear new clothes, offer prayer and greet friends and relatives. Generally no breakfast is served on this Eid and those who offer sacrifice do not eat anything until they have sacrificed the animal. Millions of animals are slaughtered all over the world on this occasion. The skins of the slaughtered animals are given to charities and the proceeds are used for welfare purposes.

Dr. Riaz Farooq

85

7

The Islamic Year and Festivals

The Islamic calendar is based on the *lunar year* and is made up of *354 days,* comprising of twelve months, where each month has twenty-nine or thirty days. The Islamic year is eleven days shorter than the *solar* year, which means festival dates move through the solar year and cannot be dated a long time in advance. Accurate prediction of dates is not possible. Religious festivals are declared at the beginning of each lunar month and therefore vary year by year. The calendar begins with the Prophet Muhammad's 🕌 (Peace Be Upon Him) emigration from Makkah to Medina in 622 and a year is known as hijri (h), for example 1300 h=1822-23 AD. The Islamic months and some memorable dates are as follows:

Islamic Months

❶ Muharram

1st Muharram is the New Year's Day of the Islamic Calendar. Ashura is the 10th Muharram and is regarded a holy day in the memory of martyrdom of Imam Hussain ibn Ali, the grandson of the Prophet Muhammad 🕌 (PBUH) who died at Kerbela in 680 AD.

❷ Saffar

Hazrat-e Ali (RA) married Hazrat-e Fatima (RA), (the daughter of the Prophet Muhammad 🕌 (PBUH) in the latter days of Safar 2 AH.

❸ Rabi Ul-Awwal

Milad Al Nabi is the celebration of the birthday of the Prophet Muhammad 🕌 (PBUH) and is celebrated on the 12th Rabi Ul-Awal.

❹ Rabi Ul-Sani

11th Rabi Ul-Sani is the anniversary of Abdul-Qadir Gilani, Sufi of Islam.

❺ Jamaadi Ul-Awwal

The Prophet Muhammad 🕌 (PBUH) married his first beloved wife, Hazrat-e Khadijah (RA) 15 years prior to the prophethood.

❻ Jamaadi Ul-Sani

No message came from Allah to the Prophet Muhammad 🕌 (PBUH) and he was very sad during this month.

❼ Rajab

Laylat Al Miraj occurs on the 27th Rajab and it commemorates the ascension of the Prophet Muhammad 🕌 (PBUH). The Islamic code of life, especially the praying of five times was relayed to the Prophet Muhammad 🕌 (PBUH) on this night by Allah.

❽ Shábaan

Laylat Al Baraat is celebrated on the 15th Shabaan and is known as the 'Night of Forgiveness'. It is believed that Allah will determine life and destinies are fixed by Allah for the coming year on this night (Budget day). It is also known by Shab-E Barat.

❾ Ramadan

The month of fasting.

Laylat Al Qadr is known as the 'Night of Destiny' and occurs on the 27th Ramadan. It marks the first revelation of the Qur'ân on the earth to Prophet Muhammad 🕌 (PBUH) by Allah.

Calendar 2005 — 1425-1426 *Hijri*

January — *Dhu al-Qa'dah / Dhu al-Hijjah*

Mon	Tue	Wed	Thu	Fri	Sat	Sun
31					1	2
3	4	5	6	7	8	9
10	11	12	13	14	15	16
17	18	19	20	21	22	23
24	25	26	27	28	29	30

February — *Dhu al-Hijjah / Muharram 1425*

Mon	Tue	Wed	Thu	Fri	Sat	Sun
	1	2	3	4	5	6
7	8	9	10	11	12	13
14	15	16	17	18	19	20
21	22	23	24	25	26	27
28						

March — *Muharram / Safar*

Mon	Tue	Wed	Thu	Fri	Sat	Sun
	1	2	3	4	5	6
7	8	9	10	11	12	13
14	15	16	17	18	19	20
21	22	23	24	25	26	27
28	29	30	31			

April — *Safar / Rabi al-Awwal*

Mon	Tue	Wed	Thu	Fri	Sat	Sun
				1	2	3
4	5	6	7	8	9	10
11	12	13	14	15	16	17
18	19	20	21	22	23	24
25	26	27	28	29	30	

May — *Rabi al-Awwal / Rabi al-Thani*

Mon	Tue	Wed	Thu	Fri	Sat	Sun
30	31					1
2	3	4	5	6	7	8
9	10	11	12	13	14	15
16	17	18	19	20	21	22
23	24	25	26	27	28	29

June — *Rabi al-Thani / Jumaada al-awal*

Mon	Tue	Wed	Thu	Fri	Sat	Sun
		1	2	3	4	5
6	7	8	9	10	11	12
13	14	15	16	17	18	19
20	21	22	23	24	25	26
27	28	29	30			

Eid-ul-Adha 20 Jan; 1st of Muharram 10 Feb; Milad-un-Nabi 21 Apr

tel 0845 130 8990 ◆ mail@islamic-aid.com ◆ www.islamic-aid.com

Islamic Aid

Calendar 2005 — 1425-1426 *Hijri*

July — *Jumaada al-awal / Jumaada al-Thani*

Mon	Tue	Wed	Thu	Fri	Sat	Sun
				1	2	3
4	5	6	7	8	9	10
11	12	13	14	15	16	17
18	19	20	21	22	23	24
25	26	27	28	29	30	31

August — *Jumada al-Thani / Rajab*

Mon	Tue	Wed	Thu	Fri	Sat	Sun
29	30	31				
1	2	3	4	5	6	7
8	9	10	11	12	13	14
15	16	17	18	19	20	21
22	23	24	25	26	27	28

September — *Rajab / Shaban*

Mon	Tue	Wed	Thu	Fri	Sat	Sun
			1	2	3	4
5	6	7	8	9	10	11
12	13	14	15	16	17	18
19	20	21	22	23	24	25
26	27	28	29	30		

October — *Shaban / Ramadan*

Mon	Tue	Wed	Thu	Fri	Sat	Sun
31					1	2
3	4	5	6	7	8	9
10	11	12	13	14	15	16
17	18	19	20	21	22	23
24	25	26	27	28	29	30

November — *Ramadan / Shawwal*

Mon	Tue	Wed	Thu	Fri	Sat	Sun
	1	2	3	4	5	6
7	8	9	10	11	12	13
14	15	16	17	18	19	20
21	22	23	24	25	26	27
28	29	30				

December — *Shawwal / Dhu al-Qa'dah*

Mon	Tue	Wed	Thu	Fri	Sat	Sun
			1	2	3	4
5	6	7	8	9	10	11
12	13	14	15	16	17	18
19	20	21	22	23	24	25
26	27	28	29	30	31	

Mirajun Nabi 1 Sep; 1st Ramadan 4 Oct; Eidul Fitr 2 Nov

tel 0845 130 8990 ◆ mail@islamic-aid.com ◆ www.islamic-aid.com

Islamic Aid

⬆ *A calendar produced by Islamic Aid (Islamic months are shown in green).*

⑩ Shawwal

Eid Al-Fitr, a festival at the end of fasting and 1st of Shawwal.

⑪ Dhu Al-Qa'dah

Allah promised Moses (PBUH) after thirty or forty nights, after which he was to go to Mount Sinai, where he would be given the law by which he would govern his people and revealed Taurat (The Old Testament).

Prophets Ibrāhīm and Ishmāîl (Peace Be Upon Both Of Them) carried up the pillars of the Baitul Haram (House of Allah, it means building of Káaba).

⑫ Dhu Al-Hijjah

The month of Pilgrimage (Hajj) to Makkah 10th – 12th Dhul Hijja, 9th Hajj and 10th Eid Al-Adha.

Muslims celebrate several religious and cultural events. These festivals are celebrated by families, communities and Muslim societies throughout the world. Each celebration has both a material and spiritual significance. The two main religious festivals celebrated by every Muslim throughout the world are Eid Al-Fitr and Eid Al-Adha. The social meaning of Eid is joyful festival. Some cultural events are celebrated in some countries, but not others. For example, Basant (Harvest), students' day and Jashn-e-Nowrouze (New Year celebration) are annual events which are celebrated in South Asia. Various celebrations have been supported by Birmingham City Council such as Eid Mela and Lok Mela.

Henna, the dye, plays a very important role in cultural and religious festivals such as Eid Al-Fitr at the end of Ramadan and weddings. No celebration seems complete without girls having patterns done with hennah. Henna symbolises prosperity, fertility, happiness, joy, fortune and beauty. First used in the Near East and South Asia, henna art is now popular around the world. Henna is a common name for a small shrub and the leaves of the henna plant are the source of a red-brown dye widely used for body art. The orange-red dye produced from its leaves is used extensively as a rinse to impart a reddish colour to hair. Women of Muslim countries use the dye to stain the nails, tips of their fingers, and parts of their feet; or make floral designs on hands, arms and feet. Men of these countries use the dye to colour their beards. Henna contains agents which cool the part of body where henna has been applied.

Aasma Nazir

↑ *Tahmeena Parvez, a henna artist, applying a henna design on young Muslim girl's hand.*
← *Henna painting at Eid Milan Meena Bazaar 2001, Symphony Hall, Broad Street, Birmingham.*

8

Muslim Life

Social Manners and Morals

Islam forbids any action which infringes on the rights of others or harms oneself. Forbidden to Muslims are dishonesty, theft, murder, suicide, bribery, forgery, interest and usury, gambling, consumption of alcohol or pork, backbiting, gossiping, slandering, hoarding, destruction of property, cruelty to animals, adultery or fornication. Islam condemns enmity, back-biting, slander, blasphemy, ridicule, offensive names, suspicion and arrogance.

While forbidding these things, Islam enjoins upon mankind the use of all clean, healthy and useful things, and asks us not to deprive our bodies of clean food and healthy recreation. Islam also encourages marriage and stable family life, modesty, generosity, hospitality, respect for parents, honourable treatment of women and helping those in need. Islam believes in decency and good manners. Keeping one's promise, truthfulness, justice, fair play, helping the poor, respect for parents, teachers and elders, love for the children and good relations with one's neighbours are the most valued virtues of a Muslim.

Marriage is the basis of family life in Islam. It is a solemn contract between a bridegroom and a bride. Parents, with the consent of the boy and the girl, generally arrange Muslim marriages.

The principles of Islam provide practical guidelines to protect and uphold individual and collective freedoms, justice and welfare in all spheres of human activity including social, economic and political life. For Muslims, mosques provide the best place for learning and working towards the Islamic principles.

Names and Identity

In Islam it is very important that each human being should be known according to their family, origin and culture. Therefore all Muslim children are normally given Islamic names, which could be either one of the 99 names of Allah, one of the 99 names of the Prophet Muhammad ﷺ (Peace Be Upon Him) or any other name of good meaning. These are followed by family names or surnames.

Diet

Muslims have a varied diet which includes vegetables, fish, poultry, agricultural products and meat but the meat must be Halal. The meaning of Halal is pure. The meat slaughtered according to Islamic tradition is known as Halal meat and food that is not Halal is called Haraam (unlawful). Islam does not allow the consumption of Haraam food. A Muslim is not allowed to consume:

- Dead animals (due to disease and natural causes)
- Animals slaughtered without invoking the name of Allah
- Animals strangled to death
- Pigs
- Carnivorous animals
- Animals devoured by wild beasts
- The blood of an animal

Alcohol is also strictly prohibited under Islamic law.

Dress (Libas)

A Muslim is required to cover his or her body properly and decently, but no particular style of dress is recommended. Simplicity and modesty are encouraged and dress expressing arrogance is disliked. The style of dress depends on local custom

and climatic conditions. Individuals in different Muslim societies wear different types of dress. For example, Arabs wear long shirts and South Asians wear full trousers and shirts down to their knees: the salwaar and kameez. A scarf or hijab is used by females to cover their hair and faces.

◐ *Muslim girls wearing the hijab.*
◓ *Muslim girl reciting the Qur'ån, whilst wearing appropriate Muslim dress (photographed by Nick Hedges).*

◓ *Colourful bangles.*
◓ *Palestinian dress dating from about 1900 to 1930, Southall Collection [Source: Birmingham Museums & Art Gallery].*

Death and Burials

Death is accepted as inevitable in Islam. When someone dies, according to Islam, mourning should not be more than three days. During this period, the family of the deceased is visited regularly by relatives and friends. The body is taken to a mosque or Janazah Gah (funeral ground) for funeral prayer. Islam does not permit women to accompany remains to graveyards and burials. For burials in Birmingham there are graveyards in Handsworth, Kings Heath and Selly Oak where separate areas are reserved for Muslim burials.

When one hears the death of another, the following duah is recited.

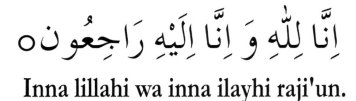

اِنَّا لِلّٰهِ وَ اِنَّا اِلَيْهِ رَاجِعُوْنَ۰

Inna lillahi wa inna ilayhi raji'un.

'To Allah belongs what he took, and to Him belongs what he gave.'

Here are a few reasons why Muslim recite Inna Lillahi Wa Inna Ilayhi Raji'un:

1. When one incurs a loss of something, one recites this duah to seek Allah's help in finding their lost belonging.
2. When one is shocked to hear certain news.

Aasma Nazir

⊕ *Cumalla Shon's grave at Lodge Hill Cemetary, Selly Oak, Birmingham.*
⊕ *Muslim grave stones at the Lodge Hill Cemetary, Selly Oak, Birmingham.*

9

Women's Rights and Responsibilities in Islam

In the West, generally, when we talk about women in Islam, we seldom go beyond a few clichés that neither do justice to women nor to Islam. At worse, the attitude is either chauvinistic or downright condescending.

Islam is, perhaps, the only religion which has treated women as beings in their own right and given them an impressive array of claims. These include free will in their choice of husbands, easy divorce, economic independence through inheritance both from father and husband, good treatment from the latter and education facilities on a par with those available to their brothers. This is in consensus with the Qur'ânic teachings which state that both male and female have been created from a single soul and both have equal rights.

Similarly, as the Qur'ân allows a man to have four wives at a time it lays down such stringent rules for equal treatment that it becomes impossible for an ordinary man to adhere to them and yet indulge in multiple marriages.

Islam teaches that both men and women were created to worship Allah. Although there are separate defined roles for both men and women, it is the Creator who defines these roles. In Islam, views concerning women are based on divine guidance and by the teachings of the Blessed Prophet Muhammad ﷺ (PBUH).

For the purpose of this book, these rights, which a Muslim woman has, will be examined briefly, including aspects relating to personal law, marriage, polygamy, divorce, inheritance, economics, employment, politics, adoption and education.

Children

In Islam every child's life is sacred. Allah especially orders the kind and just treatment of daughters.

The Mother

Islam teaches kindness to parents and in particular to the mother because she bears the child from one hardship to another, through the difficulties of pregnancy and childhood. When a woman becomes a mother in Islam, her seat of honour and dignity becomes extra special. However, many women nowadays feel that motherhood is not considered to be a 'career' that brings in financial gains and fulfilment. A mother plays a substantial part in the way a whole generation is educated, guided and trained. It requires skill and professionalism, commitment, care, devotion and dedication. In Islam it is more important to shape the future generation before pursuing a career outside.

Education

A woman has the same rights to pursue knowledge as men. History is witness to Muslim women's contribution to civilisation in various professions, for example in teaching and medicine.

Economics

The economic rights of women were denied before Islam and in secular cultures up to as late as the twentieth century. However, over fourteen centuries ago, Islam gave women the right to personal ownership of property and wealth, with the right to lease, buy and sell any portion of property independently. According to Islam, the women's right to her money, real estate or other property is acknowledged and this right does not change when she gets married.

Employment

Islam gives women the same work rights as men, as long as her important role as a mother and wife are not neglected. Without her, the future generation would lack the healthy moral conscience that is needed for the success and stability of any individual and community. Muslim women are free to pursue employment if they are able to, and if married, with the agreement of their husband.

Politics

Study of Islamic history informs us of women's political rights in Islam. Women have always had the same rights as men, to be elected, nominated to political office and to participate in all public affairs.

Marriage

Women have the right to choose their marriage partner and the marriage must have their free consent. Furthermore, a widow or a divorcee may marry whoever she wishes. Upon entering marriage, women are also entitled to retain their maiden name; this is symbolic of their unique identity. Islam, additionally, gives the women the right to mahr (marriage gift). The wife's wealth does not transfer to the wife's in-laws, father or husband but is entirely at the disposal of the woman. The natural difference between the genders is acknowledged in Islam and the physically stronger gender is given a greater degree of responsibility concerning economic maintenance and protection. However, this responsibility does not imply superiority over the woman. Man has full responsibility for the maintenance of his family. This is not only a moral but also a legal obligation. Anything a wife earns is hers and anything her husband earns is also hers to use as she wishes.

Divorce

Not only is the woman's right to choose her husband recognised, but she can also terminate her unsuccessful marriage. Divorce is taken to be a last resort in Islam. To prevent irrational decisions being made and for the sake of a family's stability, especially where children are involved, Islam enjoins that both parties observe a waiting period of three months before a

⊙ *Extract from Discover Islam "How does Islam elevate the status of women?" [Source: Trabscin International (USA) and Taibah International Aid Association, 1997].*

divorce is finalised. This enables the husband and wife to assess the situation rationally and then make a decision, and also another reason is to ensure that she is not expecting a child. If divorce is unavoidable, Allah instructs the husband to depart from his wife peacefully with no malice. The dowry (mahr) and other gifts he may have given to her cannot be taken back.

Inheritance

Islam gives women the right of inheritance, unlike in some cultures, where women themselves are considered objects to be inherited. A woman is allotted a share of inheritance and this is hers to retain and manage. No one can lay any claim to this including her father or her husband. The method of division of inheritance is clearly laid down in the Qur'ân. A general rule is that the woman's share is one half of the man's share. This may seem unfair, but this variation in inheritance is consistent with the variation in the financial responsibilities for men and women. The husband is fully responsible for the maintenance of his wife and children, a man is justly allotted a larger share. The woman, by divine right, is completely free from all financial responsibility and is maintained by her father or brother or husband as the case may be.

Women's Rights

Islam has accorded women's rights which we take for granted now, but were given by Allah to women over 1400 years ago. Islam offers women dignity, justice and protection which have long remained out of their reach. If we look at any other civilisation in history, we will not find women playing such a major role in its establishment. Islam is the only religion which, in terms of its transmission, establishment and support, was based upon the efforts of women. This is a historical matter which is not open to interpretation, it is a fact. Other women of the early Islamic period also owned land and property, cultivated crops, produced handicrafts, bought and sold goods. Some were skilled in medicine and attended the wounded during battles; some even fought in battles themselves.

This brief glance at women's status in Islam, uncovers the respectability, dignity, purity, and favours created for women. Far from struggling in aggressive campaigns for mere acknowledgment of her existence, women in Islam are effortlessly awarded liberties and privileges from their Lord, which must therefore be respected and adhered to by men.

Furkhandah J Sindhu

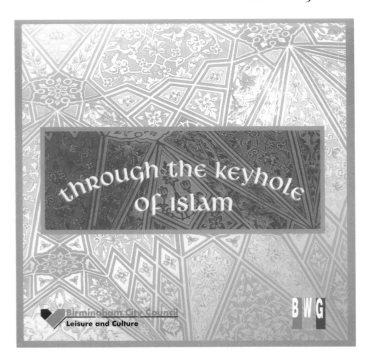

⬆ *To develop community harmony, a leaflet 'Through the Keyhole of Islam' was produced by Aasma Nazir on behalf of the Black Workers Group, Leisure and Culture, Birmingham City Council after the 9/11 atrocity.*

Image Gallery 2
Art and Artefacts

◐ *Káaba door – with two heart shaped door handles and a lock with "LA ILAHA ILA ALLAH" inscribed on it.*

⬆ *This is a Nieen runner,
having a rich pattern with a
traditional design of flower
medallions and a floral border.
It is made of the best quality
lambs' wool, silk and finely
spun cotton as the base.*

⬅ *Islamic calligraphy (Sūrah Al
Ikhlās, Al Falaq, Al
Nas and Duah) on a metal
plaque made in Egypt.*

⬇ *Iranian rug.*

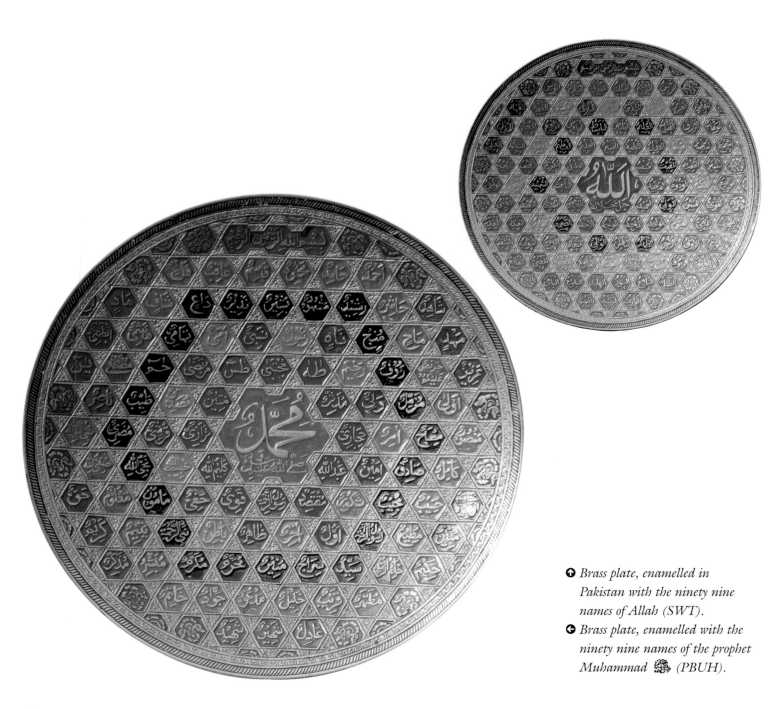

⬆ *Brass plate, enamelled in Pakistan with the ninety nine names of Allah (SWT).*

⬅ *Brass plate, enamelled with the ninety nine names of the prophet Muhammad ﷺ (PBUH).*

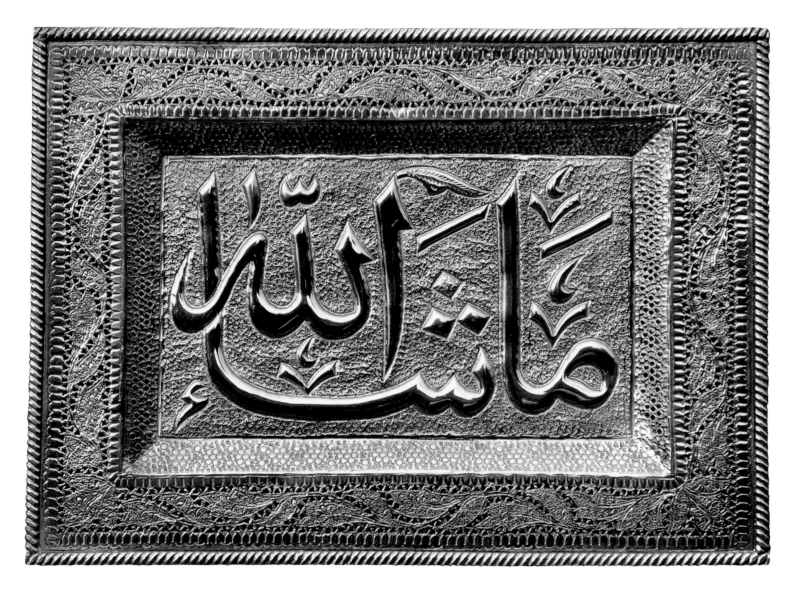

⬆ *Islamic calligraphy 'mashá allah' (What God wills) engraved on copper with cut-work designs.*

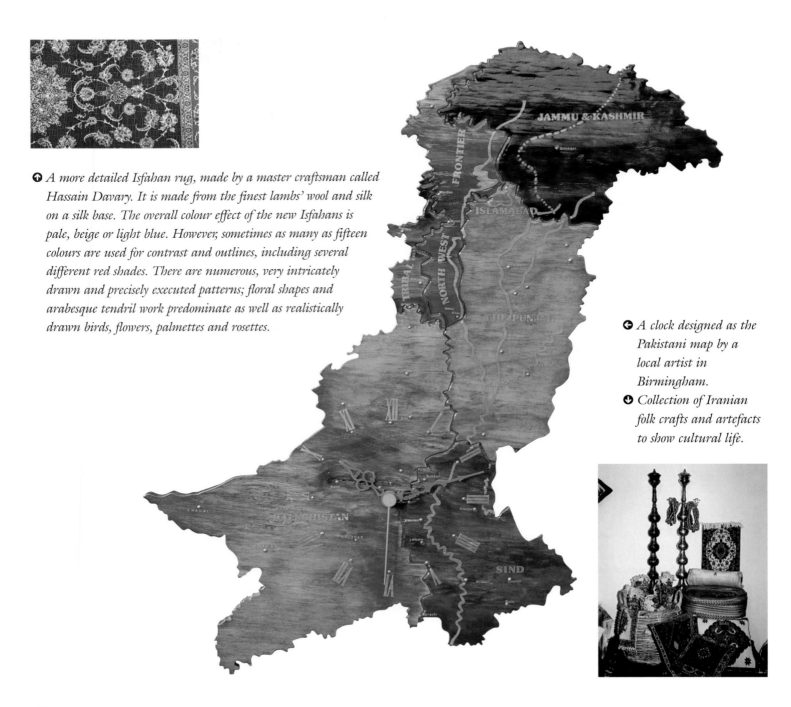

⬆ *A more detailed Isfahan rug, made by a master craftsman called Hassain Davary. It is made from the finest lambs' wool and silk on a silk base. The overall colour effect of the new Isfahans is pale, beige or light blue. However, sometimes as many as fifteen colours are used for contrast and outlines, including several different red shades. There are numerous, very intricately drawn and precisely executed patterns; floral shapes and arabesque tendril work predominate as well as realistically drawn birds, flowers, palmettes and rosettes.*

⬅ *A clock designed as the Pakistani map by a local artist in Birmingham.*

⬇ *Collection of Iranian folk crafts and artefacts to show cultural life.*

⬆ *Enamelled Brass ewer (Aftaba).*

Engraving is defined as the art of carving delicate designs on metal and in Pakistan this art has always been done in the Iranian method. Engraving is done on different metals such as copper, brass, silver, gold and also some alloys. To engrave, first the back side of the work is covered by tar to prevent the work from getting distorted as a result of hammering and the pressure of the chisel. Then the chosen design is transferred onto the work by a tool called a 'Nimbor'. The main lines are engraved, different patterns being cut afterwards by the use of different sorts of chisels on the surface of the work. Sometimes, if necessary, or according to his taste and interest, the artisan proceeds to reticulate, stone-set, gold block and silver block the product.

⬅ *Brass ewer (Aftaba).*

● *Small Tabriz rug. Lambs' wool with silk details on the flowers, on a cotton base. The cotton base enables the skilled craftsmen to create much finer knots and details in the patterns, a silk base would be even finer.*

● *Brass candle cover with cut work.*

● *Hand printed cotton tableware, produced by hand in Iran in various patterns and sizes used for tables, walls and covering furniture.*

⬆ *A top of the range rug from Isfahan, made by a master craftsman called Hassain Davary, which he has signed. It is made of the finest lambs' wool and silk on a silk base with blues, pinks and beige on a light cream background.*

⬅ *Colourful bangles on a wooden stand.*

⬇ *Crafted picture frame.*

⬆ *Copper embossed water glass.*
➡ *Silver embossed pot usually used for holding drinks.*

↑ *Islamic calligraphy engraved on brass and wood.*

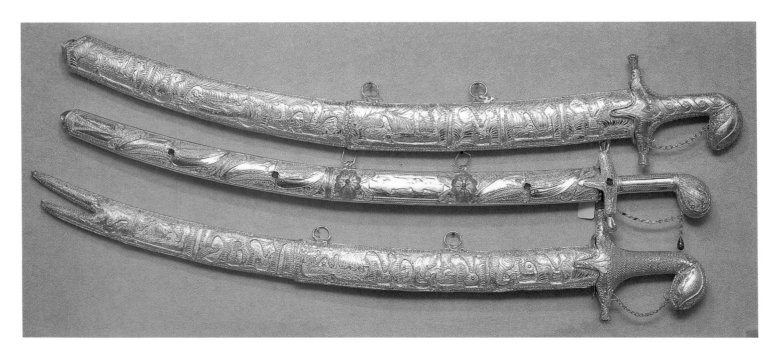

↑ Swords, usually donated to Hazrat Ali's Swords (4th Khalifah).

↱ Brass crafts engraved with Allah's name; a sword set used in wars before the nineteenth century.

↓ Islamic calligraphy engraved on brass and wood.

Islamic calligraphy (shahadah) on papyrus paper by Abdul Aziz, Cairo, Egypt. Papyrus is the oldest writing material in existence today, dating back at least 5,000 years. The very word 'paper' is derived from its name.

Verses from the Qur'ān (Sūrah Al Ikhlās); hand painted papyrus by Abdul Aziz, Cairo, Egypt.

➲ *Islamic calligraphy engraved on brass.*

➥ *Brass craft drink set containing a jug and six glasses.*

⬆ *Bakhoor (laban burner) carved.*
⬅ *Brass laban (perfume) burner.*
⬇ *Bakhoor (laban burner) carved.*

↑ Wooden craft: a tanga is a horse-drawn carriage. The traditional tanga is used in some areas of the UK but it is most popular in regions of Asia for income earning purposes. This artefact represents the cultural heritage of many cultures.

↑ Wooden craft: the traditional oilrig extracts oil essence such as almond, olive and coconut oil. As most villages in Pakistan continue with the rural way of life the oilrig is still widely used by many people. The wooden craft is both decorative and functional. It is significant in enabling us to learn how people lived before technological advancement, when discovery and development were at a very basic level.

↑ Collection of Pakistani folk crafts to show cultural life.

◔ Brass zallah (Arabic Qawa – herbal tea pot).

↑ Wooden craft: intricately hand carved, lacquered doll, reminiscent of the traditional dress of the Pathan woman. Her dress is layered with traditional designs and is indicative of fine craftsman-ship and embroidery.

↥ *Image of an Old Book by Iranian artist Mohsen Keiany.*

↪ *Image of an Old Battle by Iranian artist Mohsen Keiany.*

○ *A beautiful rug from the city of Nieen, a good example of a historical Islamic design. It is a very high quality rug and has a classification of 3 lar (3 fine strands twisted for the base yarn), being made of fine lambs' wool with silk for details and a fine cotton base.*

○ *Central design of an Isfahan rug.*

○ *Wooden Craft: A traditionally wooden crafted mirror with opening wooden doors.*

○ *Wooden carpet weaving easel, holding a piece of rug.*

Section C
Cultural Enrichment

1

Cultural Enrichment: Introduction

These articles, written by Muslim and non-Muslim individuals, provide a snapshot of Muslim cultural influences. This section is not supposed to be comprehensive – there is more that could have been written about art, architecture, textiles, poetry, literature or science – but will give the reader a flavour of the richness of the Muslim cultural contribution to our society.

Culture is an essential part of everyone's life where people engage in experiences which derive from their countries of origin. Muslim culture has been influenced by geography and Islamic philosophy, particularly the Sufi tradition of Islamic mysticism, where links have been made between poetry and other cultural activities. One Western author, Annemarie Schimmel, in her introduction to *As Through a Veil* writes that the mystical aspects of Islam understandably appealed more to non-

○ *Decorative, hand made Lanterns and Qindeels (chandeliers made of brass and coloured glass)usually used for either candles or oil.*

○ *A very high quality rug from Isfahan. Made of the best quality lambs' wool on silk or cotton base.*

Muslim readers than its legal and dogmatic aspects. The poetry of the Persian poet, Maulana Jalaluddin Rumi, was particularly attractive. The Scottish clergyman William Hastie regarded his poetry as an antidote to Omar Khayyam's frivolous verses.

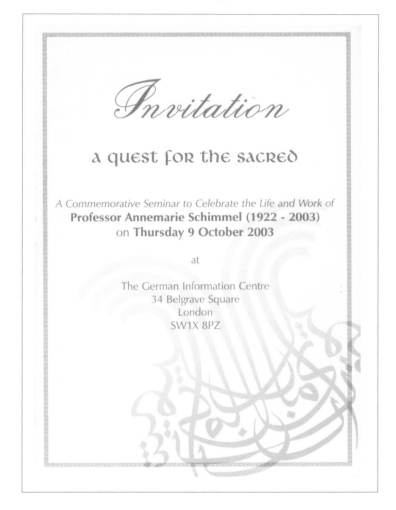

Invitation

a quest for the sacred

A Commemorative Seminar to Celebrate the Life and Work of
Professor Annemarie Schimmel (1922 - 2003)
on **Thursday 9 October 2003**

at

The German Information Centre
34 Belgrave Square
London
SW1X 8PZ

⊕ *Leaflet – A commemorative seminar to celebrate the Life and Work of Professor Annemarie Schimmel (1922 -2003) by the Iqbal Academy UK in partnership with the German Embassy, London.*

After an introduction to Sufism, which explains its relationship to Islam, there are several articles on music – we begin with an academic article on Music in Sufism followed by articles which explore Islamic musical tradition. There is an article on musical instruments played in Asian, Persian and Middle East villages and one which explores the history of Asian music in Birmingham. Music is naturally followed by folk dancing, which is part of the traditional cultures. We move onto sport such as cricket, *Gulli Danda* and *Kabaddi* followed by traditional crafts such as rug making. An architectural study looks at the minaret as a symbol of sacredness in Islam.

The final sections explore sources and collections and activities relating to Muslim culture and heritage which are held at Birmingham City Archives, Birmingham Museums & Art Gallery and the University of Birmingham.

Alison Gove-Humphries

2

Sufism: an Introduction

Tasawwuf is the Arabic word for Sufism which is generally known to be the inner, mystical, or psycho-spiritual aspect of Islam. Many Muslims and non-Muslims believe that Sufism is outside the sphere of Islam. However, Seyyed Hossein Nasr, one of the foremost scholars of Islam, argues that Sufism is simply the name for the inner or esoteric dimension of Islam.

The essence of Sufism practice is that the Sufi (practioners of Sufism) relinquish to Allah, in love, over and over again. This involves acceptance with love at each moment of one's consciousness (one's perceptions, thoughts, and feelings, as well as one's sense of self) as gifts of Allah or, more precisely, as the appearance of Allah.

Sufis see themselves as being on a spiritual journey towards Allah and guiding other spiritual travellers. To express the status of consciousness experienced during this journey, Sufis have produced a massive treasure of literature. This journey is referred to as *tariqah* (the path). All Muslims believe that they are on the pathway to Allah and will become close to Allah in Jannah (Paradise) after death at the 'Final Judgment Day', whereas Sufis believe that it is possible to become close to Allah and to experience this closeness whilst one is alive.

Since Sufis have begun to speak about Sufism, they have defined it in many different ways. Following is the information about how some Sufis defined Sufism in the ninth and tenth centuries (AD) from Nicholson, R., ed., *Kitab al-Luma'* (The Book of Flashes) pp. 34-35.

► Muhammed ibn Ali al-Qassab: Sufism consists of noble behaviour that is made manifest at a noble time on the part of a noble person in the presence of a noble people. Sufism is that you should be with Allah without any attachment.

► Ruwayam ibn Ahmad: Sufism consists of abandoning oneself to Allah in accordance with what Allah wills.

► Samnun ibn `Umar al-Muhibb: Sufism is that you should not possess anything nor should anything possess you.

► Abu Muhammad al-Jariri: Sufism consists of entering every exalted quality and leaving behind every despicable quality.

► Amr ibn `Uthman al-Makki: Sufism is that at each moment the servant should be in accord with what is most appropriate at that moment.

► Ali ibn `Abd al-Rahim al-Qannad: Sufism consists of extending a 'spiritual station' and being in constant union.

R. A. Nicholson's introduction to Sufism in *The Mystics of Islam* (1914) states that: 'Sufism, the religious philosophy of Islam, is described in the oldest extant definition as 'the apprehension of divine realities',' and although referring to it as 'Islamic mysticism,' he still maintains the popular idea that Sufism was largely the product of diverse philosophical and spiritual influences, including Christian, Neoplatonic, and others. He further states that it is 'a subject so vast and many-sided that several large volumes would be required to do it anything like justice.'

More than 35 years later his student, A. J. Arberry, in his brief introduction to the subject, *Sufism* (1950), similarly states that Sufism is 'the name given to the mysticism of Islam' and 'the mystical movement of an uncompromising monotheism.' It was this author who first maintained that, although Sufism was the recipient of many influences from Neoplatonic and other sources, it was in essence derived from the Qur'ân and Prophetic (Muhammadan) tradition, and attempted to view 'the movement from within as an aspect of Islam, as though these other factors which certainly determined its growth did not exist.' This approach became generally accepted and was echoed by later scholars.

Colour of the Earth,
oil on canvas by
Iranian artist
Mohsen Keiany.

117

Sufism and Remembrance (Dhikr) of Allah

The Qur'ân directs Muslims to remember Allah, whose reality covers and permeates both the visible and non-visible worlds. Sufis have developed this into the exemplary Sufi practice of silent and vocal *dhikr* (remembrance).

Sufism and Love

The Sufi follows the path towards Allah first and foremost by means of love. For the Sufi who is enraptured with the love of Allah, all of existence is extraordinarily beautiful. In contrast, one who is not in love with Allah to this degree will not see what is so astounding about existence.

Shaykhs, Sufi Orders, and Shrines

Selected Sufis	Sufi Orders and their Shaykhs
Hasan al-Basri	Malamatiya
Rabi'a al-Adawiya	Yasawiya – Ahmet Yasawi
Bayazid-i Bistami	Kubrawiya (and Oveyssi) – Najm al-Din Kubra
Sahl ibn 'Abdallah al-Tustari	Qadiriya – 'Abd al-Qadir Jilani
Mansur al-Hallaj	Rifa'iya – Ahmet Rifa'i
Abu 'l-Hasan Kharaqani	Mevleviye – Jalal al-Din Rumi
Abu Sa'id Abu al-Khayr	Bektashiye – Haji Bektash Veli
Khwajah 'Abdallah Ansari	Naqshbandiya – Baha' al-Din Naqshband
Abu Hamid al-Ghazali	Ni'matallahiya – Shah Ni'matallah Vali
'Ayn al-Qudat Hamadani	Bayramiye – Haji Bayram Veli
Ruzbihan-i Baqli	Chishtiya – Mu'in al-Din Chishti
Ibn 'Arabi	Shadhiliya – Abu al-Hasan al-Shadhili
Yunus Emre	Khalwatiya – 'Umar al-Khalwati
	Tijaniya – Ahmad al-Tijani
	Muridiyya – Ahmadu Bamba
	Qalandariya

Aasma Nazir

Reference:

1. www.arches.uga.edu/~godlas/Sufism.html

↩ *Kocch, oil on canvas by Iranian artist Mohsen Keiany.*

3

The Musical Tradition in Sufism

Sufism (more properly, *tasawwuf* in Arabic, cognate with *safa*: purity) – also known as Islamic mysticism in the West – originated soon after the advent of Islam (610 AD), initially as a reaction to the worldliness and pomp of the Umayyad kings (661-749) of Damascus. Its aim was to find the truth, divine love and spiritual cleanliness through direct personal experience of God. To achieve these goals a number of mystical paths (*tariqas*) were followed, involving ascetic practices (e.g. poverty and fasting) and continuous repetition (*dhikr*) of divine names and epithets: e.g. *Allah, Allah*; *haqq, haqq* (reality or truth), *hu', hu'* (He). In these practices, *sama'* (spiritual audition) and *wajd* (ecstasy) played an important role. Devotional music was a highly significant component of this spiritual experience, leading to the mystical state (*hal*: crudely, trance). It must, however, be pointed out that in early Arabic works – derived from and extending the Greek treatises on the subject – the word *musiqi* was confined to the theory and art of music-making or composition of melodies; the product itself was called *ghina* (lyric, song) or *alhan* (melodies).

Whether the performance, of music (or dance: *raqs*) is allowed by religious law (*Shari'ah*) in Islam has been the subject of debate for many centuries in all Muslim countries – but Sufis were amongst the first to perform both genres. The spectrum of opinion ranged from authorities who held music to be illegal and sinful; through those who allowed it under certain conditions; to yet others who considered music to be, in fact, laudable and a means of creating spiritual uplift, inner enlightenment and ecstasy. As an outstanding Islamic philosopher and thinker, al-Ghazali (d.1111), wrote in defence of

Sama' (spiritual audition): "Hearts are treasuries (*makhzans*) of jewels – and the only way to extract their treasures is through the flint and steel of *sama'*."

Another Sufi master, Abu Hafs Suhrawardi (d.1234), stated that *sama'* is 'the audition of sound, and the realisation of ecstasy, *without* shattering the inward silence' (silence and stillness being one of the foremost points of etiquette in Sufism). True *Sama'*, moreover, demanded three other imperatives: proper time, place and company – all interpreted in a spiritual sense; namely when the heart is clean; the place is serene and holy; and the company is of '*ikhwan as-safa*' (brethren of purity and piety). In such circumstances only was spiritual audition (and *raqs*) lawful.

As to *raqs* (mystical dancing), they are the most well known of Muslim mysticism. Mevlana Jalal al-Din Rumi (1207-73) wrote the great didactic poem in Persian, the '*Mathnawi*' (containing about 26,000 couplets). With this poem is associated the tradition of the 'whirling dervishes' of Turkey, who sought ecstasy through an elaborate dancing ritual, accompanied by enchanting music.

Over the centuries, the theory and practice of Sufism underwent profound changes – especially through the interaction of Islamic thought and beliefs with outside civilisations and ideologies with which the Muslims came into contact. Important amongst these were the Greek and Byzantine civilisations of the Near East, the Zoroastrian religion of Iran, and the Hindu philosophy of ancient India. This gave Sufi tenets and practices a much greater universality and tolerance of other beliefs and systems of thought.

The emphasis now was on *ma'rifa* – an inner knowledge of reality, purity of soul, seeking after divine love and truth – as opposed to external observances of rituals, letter of the law (whether sacred or man-made), strict adherence to customs and modes of behaviour. It must be emphasised that many or

⬆ *Harmony of the Earth (Mystical Dancing), oil on canvas by Iranian artist Mohsen Keiany.*

most schools of Sufism do hold that beliefs and practices enjoined by the Qur'ân and the Prophet Muhammad ﷺ (PBUH) must be obeyed.

Sufism has had a strong hold in the Indian subcontinent (the areas now occupied by Pakistan, India and Bangladesh) for the last 1000 years. It is, in fact, through the teachings and practice of some outstanding Sufi saints that Islam originally spread, and took such a firm hold, throughout India – starting from the North, but spreading fast to the West, the East and the South of the subcontinent. Outstanding among these Sufi saints were Shaykh Ali Hujwiri (also known as Data Ganj-bakhsh) of Lahore (d.1072), Khawaja Moin-ud-Din Chishti of Ajmer (d.1236), Shaykh Baha-ud-Din Zakaria of Multan (d.1262), Baba Farid Ganj-i Shakar of Pakpatan (d.1265), and Hazrat Nizam-ud-Din Aulia of Delhi (d.1324). In order effectively to interact with the indigenous populations of India, the Sufi masters had to carry out their teachings in the local tongues. It is because of this that these languages, viz. Panjabi, Seraiki, Sindhi – and to some extent Urdu and Pashto – have become such rich repositories of Sufi literature, especially mystical poetry – e.g. that of Baba Farid (d.1265); Sultan Bahu (d.1691); Rahman Baba (d.1709); Shah Abdul Latif Bhitai (d.1752); and Baba Bulleh Shah (d.1752 – 58).

Most of the Sufi divines of the Indo-Pakistan subcontinent encouraged, or at least tolerated, the practice of *Sama'* and *raqs* in their *mehfils* (assemblies) – and their shrines continue to this day to be the loci of the performance of religious music – *Sama'*, including *qawwali*, recitation of *na'at* (homage to Prophet Muhammad ﷺ PBUH), *manqabat* (homage to Hadhrat Ali and the descendants of the Prophet), *kafis* (spiritual poetry), *ghazals* (lyrical compositions, often on Sufi themes) – and even mystical *raqs* (dance of ecstasy). In the performance of Sufi music, sung poetry forms an integral part of the experience. Starting chiefly from Persian masters such as Hafiz and Rumi,

the language and idiom of 'spiritual' poetry (emphasizing *ma' rifa* or inner knowledge) in all the mentioned oriental tongues became an intricate and almost indivisible amalgam of images of sacred and profane or secular love (*'ishq-i haqiqi* and *'ishq-i majazi*, respectively). Thus the rose and the nightingale, the candle and the moth, the elusive beloved and the crazed lover, the concealed beauty and the seeking eye, the mirror and the beholder: all became standard metaphors and allusive symbols of the divine as well as human love and desire for union.

The outstanding genius of Indian Sufi music and poetry was Amir Khusrow of Delhi (1253-1324), a disciple of Hadhrat Nizamud Din Aulia, 'the Sultan of all Shaykhs', whose *khanqah* (shrine) in Delhi – where he is buried, with Khusrow at his feet in a nearby grave – still attracts millions of visitors. These include both Muslims and Hindus, who come to seek his blessings to banish their afflictions and solve the 'knotty' problems (*mushkil kushai*) of their lives.

Amir Khusrow, of Turkish origin in Central Asia – and a nobleman in the court of seven kings of Delhi – was a polymath genius. He is still regarded – even in Iran – as one of the greatest Persian poets, to whom even Hafiz (d.1388) paid homage. He was probably one of the arch-founders of the language now known as Urdu, by combining elements of Persian, Arabic, Turkish and local Sanskrit-based languages of India; and he made profound contributions in the field of music. It was indeed he who married the Indian classical music (his mother is believed to have been of Hindu lineage) with the Arabic – Persian – Turkish traditions of the Muslim newcomers in the subcontinent. He thus greatly enriched and expanded the repertoire of Indian classical *ragas*, mixed and amalgamated Hindi and Persian idioms, words, rhythms and melodies, transformed and cross-bred many Indian and Central Asian (Persi-Turkic) instruments.

To Khusrow is attributed the evolution of the Greco-Persian zither or *seh-tar* (three-strings) into the modern-day *sitar*; the

● *Sufi music performed by German sufis at Symphony Hall, Broad Street, Birmingham during the Eid Milan Meena Bazaar 2002.*

transformation of the Persi-Arabic drum (*tabal*) into the Indian *dhol* (or *dholak*); the creation of the twin *tabla* drums by splitting the Indian *pakhavaj* into two – and so on. Amir Khusrow is also credited with having created the genre *qawwali* (from the Arabic, *qowl*, speech) – so popular throughout the world today (cf. Nusrat Fateh Ali Khan, the Pakistani maestro, d.1997). Innumerable additions – some well-established, some apocryphal – that the Amir made to the modes, contents and 'emotional tones' of Indian classical music – both vocal and instrumental – have made Khusrow the subject of much scholarly research and debate today.

It was with this background in mind that the discerning listener would have approached and received the presentations by the two world-renowned artists participating in the Iqbal Academy (UK)'s classical concert, Music of the East: 2000, held at the International Convention Centre in Birmingham, namely Dame Abida Parveen (vocalist, Sufi spiritual music) from Pakistan, and Ustad Sabri Khan (instrumentalist, the *Sarangi* maestro) from India.

Professor Saeed Durrani

4

Music in Muslim Societies: The Divine Chant?

⬆ *Muhammad Saeed reciting an Adhan at Birmingham Central Mosque for Friday prayer.*

Islamic music emerged both from pre-Islamic Arabian music and from contributions by Persians, Byzantines and Berbers, as well as certain Semitic nations of the Middle East. In this development, the Arabian element acted as a catalyst and, within a century, the new art was firmly established from Central Asia to the Atlantic. Such a fusion of musical styles succeeded because there were strong affinities between Arabian music and the music of the nations occupied by the expanding Arab Empire. Not all Arab-dominated areas adopted the new art; parts of Africa and the Far East, for example, retained their native musical styles. The folk music of the Berbers, Turks and Persians also remained alien to classical Islamic (or Arabian) music. The further one looks from the Nile Valley to Persia, the less one finds undiluted 'Islamic' music.

In pre-Islamic times, music was closely connected with poetry and dance. Being essentially vocal, pre-Islamic music was an emotional extension of the solemn declamation of poems in Bedouin society. After the advent of Islam, a deep change occurred in the social function of music. Emphasis was laid on music as entertainment and sensual pleasure, rather than as a source of high spiritual emotion.

Prophet Muhammad 🕌 (Peace Be Upon Him) was said to have been hostile to music and musicians of his time – yet he tolerated, indeed encouraged, functional music such as war songs, and public and private festival music. In, addition, Islam instituted the unique call to prayer (*Adhan*), chanted by the Muslims. For this task, the Prophet Muhammad 🕌 (PBUH) chose an

Abyssinian baritone with a booming voice, Bilal, who became the patron of *Mu'adhdhins* throughout the Islamic world.

Except in the Sufi brotherhood, religious music is curtailed because of the opposition of religious leaders. The orthodox religious authorities frowned upon music, with its clear association with erotic dance and drinking; and these stimulated hostile reactions.

In this controversy, three main groups emerged: (1) uncompromising purists opposed to any musical expression, except cantillation of the Qur'ân and *adhan*; (2) people favouring music, believing that there is no conflict between secular and religious music; and (3) mystical fraternities, for whom music and dance are a means towards unity with God.

These mystical fraternities in Central Asia, Persia, the Indian Subcontinent and the Far East have traditions of devotional music, which is euphoniously melodious, tuneful and harmonious, spiritually moving – and dare one add – simply divine?

Aziz Ahmed

Reference

1. Aziz Ahmed, The souvenir booklet of the Iqbal Academy, UK's 1995 International Conference on "Iqbal and the Fine Arts: The Heritage of Islamic creativity".

Nasheeds

A new era of musical tradition has emerged within the Muslim community. This has taken the form of Nasheeds and is aimed at the younger generation, even though many of the older generation also enjoy listening to such art. Nasheeds are sung by artists from all corners of the globe in various languages including English, Arabic, Turkish and Urdu. They possess meaning and try to teach Muslims different concepts, raise their awareness and increase their understanding of specific aspects and teachings of Islam.

Nasheeds take many forms, ranging from lullabies to raps and are catchy, as they are aimed at attracting younger people to listen to them and take note of what is being said. They are not referred to as "songs" because this label does not depict the essence and meaning of what Nasheeds are and their importance.

For many Muslims, it is not permissible to listen to music in Islam as music is regarded as being the instrument of the devil. The fear is that if it is listened to one may forget Allah. Thus, alternative types of music are created like Nasheeds, especially for those living in Western countries where listening to music is quite usual. It is better to listen to something that is more Islamically focussed and possesses meaning by glorifying Allah and the teachings of Islam. The only form of music that is permissible in Islam is the voice and the *Duff*; a one-sided drum. Women, however, are not allowed to sing in front of those who are not their Mahrem, or guardian. Most Nasheeds tend not to use any other music and try to adhere to the teachings of Islam.

Listening to Nasheeds is becoming increasingly popular and is a favourite alternative to conventional Western Music. Nasheed artists include Zain Bhikr, Yusuf Islam (better known as Cat Stephens before his conversion to Islam), Raihaan, Sami Yusuf and Dawud Warsby-Ali.

Furkhandah J Sindhu

⊕ *Famous Qawwal, Sabbari Brothers, Ghulam Farid Sabri and Maqbool Ahmed Sabri performing Qawwali 'Tajdar-e-Haram Ho Nighan-e-Karam' at Symphony Hall, Broad Street, Birmingham during the Eid Milan Meena Bazaar 2002.*

Musical Instruments

Most of the Muslim population comes from villages; their music has been associated with, and inspired by village life and its natural environment. Musical instruments commonly used are made of clay, hides, wood, wild reeds, pumpkins etc., which used to be easily available in the village. The *ghara* (pot to store water) and *borrindo* are ancient, simple instruments made out of clay. The *dhol* is made out of wood and animal skin and the *murli* from a gourd. The easy availability of these articles has made musical instruments accessible to all. This is one reason why our folk music has developed to the extent it has and is so widely diffused.

We may divide musical instruments into three categories:

❶ String instruments that are stroked, plucked or bowed, like the *sitar, rubab* etc.

❷ Wind instruments that are blown like the flute, *borrindo* etc.

❸ Percussion instruments that are tapped like the drums or *tablas*.

Alghoza

This twin-fluted blow instrument is also called a pava or binu. The 'male' flute or *nar* has eight equidistant holes at one end and is the drone, while the 'female' or *madi* weaves the melody on this base with twelve equidistant holes at the end. Only the upper six holes of the *madi* are played, the lower six being left free. The technique of circular breathing is often utilised in playing this instrument.

Bansuri

The *bansuri* is a flute made of a 30cm to 40cm long bamboo pipe. Six equidistant small holes are pierced through towards one end, and one larger hole in the same line towards the tip of the other end. Blowing somewhat horizontally into the larger hole produces sound, and using the fingertips on the other six holes regulates the music.

➊ *Bansuri.*

Borindo

This is a simple hollow terracotta ball with four holes, one slightly larger than the other three. It is made from soft alluvial clay. The three smaller holes are arranged in an isosceles triangular form. Blowing through the lips across the larger hole produces the sound. Fingertips are used in the smaller holes to regulate the pitch.

Chimta

This instrument is a pair of fire tongs. Larger *chimtas* were fashioned for big fires around which mystics and *faqirs* congregate at the shrines of saints and were first used by these devotees as musical instruments. The *chimta* used by performers is approximately one metre long and is played by bringing the tongs together by rhythmic pressure of the forefinger and thumb of the left hand. It is used mostly for folk and mystic songs.

➔ *Chimta.*

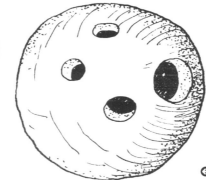

⬅ *Borindo.*
↘ *Dhol.*
⬇ *Chang.*

Dhol

The *dhol* is a double-headed outdoor drum played with a pair of wooden sticks. One stick is small with a slight curve, while the other is longer, thicker and pronouncedly curved at its end. The *dhol's* sound chamber is made from a hollow piece of a mango or shisham (dalbergia sissu) tree trunk. The heads are stretched with a membrane of specially treated goatskin. The sound of the *dhol* is loud and deep and is usually accompanied by the chimta.

Chang

Made of iron, the *chang* has an outer frame with a flexible metal strip protruding from the middle. It is played by holding it in the mouth and vibrating the metal strip with soft backward strokes of the forefinger, with the mouth acting as a sound chamber. It is also known as Persian harp or Jew's harp.

Dholak

The *dholak* is a smaller version of a *dhol* and *pakhavaj*. It is a popular percussion instrument and usually played by hand. It is mostly used for lighter forms like the *ghazal* – a light classical poetic Indian music form, associated with Muslim Northern India and the Urdu language.

● *Dholak.*

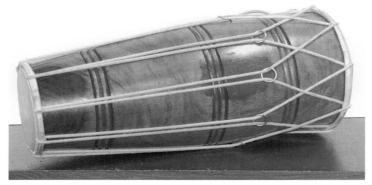

Ektara

One of the earliest examples of string instruments is the *ektara* (monochord). As its name implies, it has been traditionally a single-stringed instrument. Generally, however, it has two strings, though it is still called by its original name.

● *Ektara.*
● *Hassan Shah plays the Ghara.*

Ghara

The *ghara* is round in shape with a short neck and an opening at the top. Striking one hand on the sidewalls produces rhythms, while the other hand is hit over the mouth, producing a deep booming sound. The *ghara* is rotated slowly while playing to ensure that hitting the walls constantly at the same spot does not cause it to break. The *chimta, sitar, harmonium* or *ektara* usually accompanies the ghara.

Hassan Shah

Born in 1957 he joined his brother Rauf Ali Shah in 1971. Having a beautiful singing voice and acquiring good skills in playing the *Ghara* (which is also called Matka), Hassan became a major influence on the future development of the music. Since 1971 Hassan has been performing in major events and gatherings. He has created a new style of playing the *Ghara*, which encompasses the power of the rings and the base, and also its flexibility, which creates and defuses many moods of the *Sitar*. He has worked comfortably with Musicians visiting from Pakistan. Many young people in the UK have learnt *Ghara* from him. Hassan has recently recorded a signature tune for a local Radio programme in Worcestershire.

Harmonium

During the mid-19th century a French made, hand-pumped musical instrument was introduced into the Indian sub-continent. This was portable, reliable, easy to learn and considered to be one of the most versatile of instruments. It is usually used as an accompanying instrument for vocalists. Alexandre Debain invented the harmonium in Paris in 1842.

A harmonium consist of banks of brass reeds (metal tongues which vibrate when air flows over them), a pumping apparatus, stops for drones (some models feature a stop which causes a form of vibrato), and a keyboard. The harmonium's timbre, or sound, is similar to an accordion, but works in a critically different way. Instead of the bellows causing a direct flow of air over the reeds, an external feeder bellows inflates an internal reservoir bellows inside the harmonium, from which air escapes to vibrate the reeds. This design is similar to bagpipes as it allows the harmonium to create a continuously sustained sound. If a harmonium has multiple sets of reeds, it's possible for the second set of reeds to be tuned an octave lower and these can be activated by a stop, which means each key pressed will play two notes an octave apart. Professional harmoniums feature a third set of reeds, usually tuned an octave higher. This overall makes the sound fuller. In addition, many harmoniums feature an octave coupler, a mechanical linkage that opens a valve for a note an octave below the note being played, and a scale changing mechanism, which allows one to play in various keys while fingering the keys of one scale.

Harmoniums are made with 1, 2, 3 and occasionally 4 sets of reeds. Classical instrumentalists usually use 1-reed harmoniums, while a musician who plays for a qawwali (Islamic devotional singing) usually uses a 3-reed harmonium.

⬅ *A Harmonium being played alongside a Ghara.*

Khanjari (Daff)

This instrument is similar to the *daff* but is smaller in size and struck with the hands. The *daff* is a round wooden-framed tambourine that can be found across the whole of the Arab world, in various shapes and sizes (from 12cm to 70cm). It is made with goatskin and usually has cymbals and some decorative inlay. It is also played by the Swahili people of East Africa. A khanjari is very much like the European gypsy tambourine.

○ *Khanjari.*
○ *Daff.*

Lolly (sweet) shape drum

It is a lolly (sweet) shape drum. Two beads are attached with pieces of strings in the cross direction. It is played by holding the stick middle of both hands and rubbing them in a way that beads can hit the heads in rhythm.

○ *Lolly.*

Murli

This is a twin-fluted instrument; its upper part is a dry hollow bottle gourd, which serves as a chamber of compressed air. The flute to the left (seen from the player's side) has eight equidistant holes burnt into it and is used to play the melody, while the right-hand drone has two holes at the end, giving a choice of two drone pitches.

○ *Murli.*

Nad (Sankh)

The horn of an animal is used to make this instrument. Open at two ends, the *nad* is blown at the narrow end to produce a loud, sonorous sound. The smaller ones are called *singri*, while the larger ones are called *nad* or *nafil*. It is often used by wandering mystics, who associate it with Hazrat Ali, calling it the *nad* of Ali (*nad-I-ali*).

○ *Nad.*

Nar

This is a long, end-blown shepherd's flute slightly over 60cm in length. It is usually fashioned from a hollow reed cut so that there are seven segments in it. The word *nar* also means intestine. Air is blown into it at an oblique angle with the player also making a buzzing sound into it. A singer (*suri*), who chants ballads and songs, accompanies the *nari*.

Pakhavaj

The *pakhavaj* is a double-sided drum, which is a popular rhythm accompaniment for vocal, folk and some classical music. The left-hand side of the *pakhvaj* produces a deep mellow sound, while the right yields a shorter and harder tone. Traditionally used to accompany dances and devotional songs, it is played more with the palm than with the fingers.

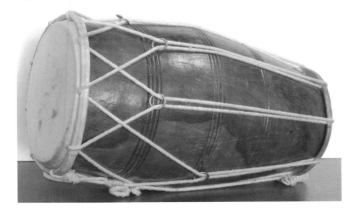

⬆ *Former Birmingham Lord Mayor, Cllr Mahmood Hussain, accompanied with drum players and Abdul Qayyum Chaudhary at Eid Milan Meena Bazaar 2002, Birmingham.*
⬅ *Pakhavaj.*

Rubab

This short-necked, plucked lute with a membrane-covered waisted body is made of mulberry wood and the membrane of goatskin.

It usually has three main playing strings made of gut (*jalau, miana*) and, more recently, nylon (*kata*), with about a dozen sympathetic strings (*tarab*) made of metal. It is played with a wooden plectrum (*shahbaz*). The *rubab* is the predecessor of the South Asian *sarod*. Folk ballads, romantic songs and popular mystic poetry are sung to the accompaniment of the *rubab*.

⬆ *Rubab.*

Sarinda

A hollow wooden body made from a single block of mulberry wood. Seven to nine steel and copper strings are tensioned over the finger-board. The *sarinda* is played with a horsehair bow (*kaman*) coated with resin. It is very similar to the folk instruments of Baluchistan, (*suroz*) and Sind (*khamach*). The *sarinda* played by the late great Pakistani folk instrumentalist Munir Sarhadi is an innovation of his father Ustad Pazir Khan who is, in living memory, the best *sarinda* player ever born.

⬆ *Sarinda.*

Sitar

Amir Khusrau invented this instrument in the fourteenth century. The sound of the *sitar* is made of a large dry hollow gourd (*kaddu*). The fingerboard is made of two pieces of wood. The neck is hollow and consists of a flat wooden fingerboard glued to a convex piece of wood. The fingerboard is mated to the gourd with another piece of wood. Nickel-plated, movable, brass frets are tied to the fingerboard with gut. Two bridges made either of bone or ivory are placed on the soundboard, a big one for the upper strings and smaller one for the sympathetic strings. A *mizrab* or steel plectrum is used for playing a *sitar*. It is made of steel wire and is worn on the forefinger of the right hand rather like a ring.

Rauf 'Ali' Shah

was born in a Rawalpindi village called Manakra in 1950. Ali emigrated to Redditch in 1965 to join his father, Arif Shah. Rauf Ali Shah brought the instruments with him in 1968, learnt to play the *Sitar*, teamed up with Abdul Warid who played the *Ghara* and began performing for friends and community events in Redditch, Birmingham, Coventry, Lye and Stourbridge.

⊙ *Rauf 'Ali' Shah playing the Sitar in Symphony Hall, Birmingham.*

Sarangi

The *sarangi* is a classical bowed string instrument. It is short in structure, with a pinched or waisted sound box. This and the fingerboard are made of one piece of wood. The resonator is covered with thin leather and the upper part with smooth wood. There is a slender bridge on the membrane and three to four guts are strung over this, passing onto the pegs. These are the melody strings. This instrument is similar to the violin.

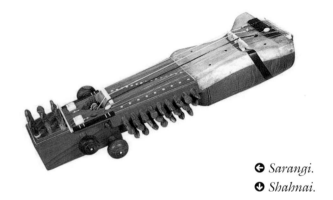

⊙ *Sarangi.*
⊙ *Shahnai.*

Shahnai

The *shahnai* is very popular instrument in Asia and played in classical styles. It is about 60cm long, conically bored in a thick expanding tube of a close-grained wood with seven fingerholes and a short flared brass bell. This instrument is used at wedding ceremonies

⬆ *Sitar and Ghara at Centenary Square, Birmingham.*

Sarod

This instrument is similar to *rabaab*. A steel plate is fitted on the fingerboard and with that the sound, unlike that of the *rabaab*, is metallic and loud.

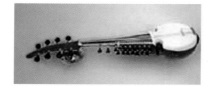

⬆ *Sarod.*

Surbahar

This is a large *sitar* with thick strings and heavy frets. It is used for *aalaap*, which is an improvisation that precedes a *dhrupad* or song.

⬆ *Surbahar.*

Tabla

These are a pair of small kettle drums. The wider drum played by the right hand is called the *duggi* while the larger drum played by the left hand is called the *dugga*. The tops of both drums are stretched with goat hide. A black circle (*siyahi*) made from iron slag powder (*loh-chur*) is glued to the centre of the stretched goatskin to control the resonance.

◔ *Tabla.*

Tanpura

This is a well-known instrument with four strings, used to provide the basic pitch. *Tan* means to spread/continue and *pura* means to fill. It is used to accompany both vocalists and instrumentalists. The size indicates whether it is to accompany the male or female voice.

Makhdoom Ahmad Chishti

References

1. www.en.wikipedia.org/wiki/Harmonium
2. Pakistan Folk Festival Brochure (Lok Virsa, Islamahad, 1988).
3. Tony Halliday, 'Insight Guides – Pakistan' (APA publications HK Ltd, Pakistan, 1992).
4. M. Harif Raza, 'Multan Past and Present' (Colourpix, Islamahad, 1988).

The late Ustad Nusrat Fateh Ali Khan's portrait.

Making Music

The Asian Broadcasting Company (ABC) was formed in 1968 and its aim was to promote Asian Culture through broadcasting amongst the Asian and local communities. This was to enable Asians to create understanding of their rich culture. It also provided musical entertainment. Saeed Zafar and Muhammad Ayyub pioneered Asian Broadcasting in Birmingham by starting an Asian Programme on Birmingham Hospital Broadcasting Network (BHBN) in 1968. This weekly programme was broadcast from the BHBN studios at Edgbaston County Cricket Ground. The first ever Asian local radio programme in Britain was started on 4th July 1971 for 15 minutes from the Pebble Mill BBC Studios on Local Radio Birmingham now known as Radio WM and it later became a weekly programme.

The first Asian Song Contest was launched in 1975 by Muhammad Ayyub to promote new talent and introduce Asian Music. He is a producer of Asian records and tapes through Oriental Star Agencies. Muhammad Ayyub came to England in 1961, aged 22 from Gujrat in Pakistan. He also produces *Gazals* recordings, which are semi-classical romantic songs. He has pioneered the work of the late Ustal Nusrat Fateh Ali Khan who is the king of *Qawwalis* which are the heart of Sufi music. Furthermore, the 1980s were a revolutionary era for Bhangra music. Young people liked Bhangra and were interested in Western instruments such as guitars and synthesisers and new combined sound tracks were introduced. Ayyub has produced and distributed more than 700 albums of famous artists who include Ustad Nusrat Fateh Ali Khan and Bally Sagoo.

Makhdoom Ahmad Chishti

⬅ *Muhammad Ayyub, proprietor of Oriental Star Agencies, with his music production of the late Ustad Nusrat Fateh Ali Khan.*

8

Dancing

Folk dancing is an integral part of many traditional cultures. People's lifestyle and feelings are reflected in their music and dances. Folk dancing is different from classical dancing. Folk dance emphasises openness and generality in its free movements, which have been developed from the folk cultures over the centuries.

Folk dances are performed at several levels in Muslim cultures. At one level, it is performed by almost everybody at weddings and festivals, for example, if they win at *Kabaddi*, people will raise their arms and start doing the *Bhangra* to the beat of the drum. The *Dhamal* is done after getting into a devotional trance, where the dance expresses the state of mind rather than the skill of the dancer. In the same way, the *Luddi* is done to share the happy occasion of a wedding with family and friends rather than showing off the mastery of dance. Folk dances usually have simple and repetitive steps. They are generally performed in groups and are rarely choreographed.

Bhangra

Bhangra is a dance of joy performed at harvest time and other celebrations in the Punjab. Vigorous arm and leg movements involving flinging arms upwards and jumping characterise the *Bhangra*. Loud sounds accompany the rhythmic drumbeats of the *Bhangra*.

Chap

Chap is performed in a circle, with all participants clapping. A musician (*lobri*) stands in the middle with a bow instrument (*saruz*). The word "chap" refers to the clapping. The variations are according to the number of claps for each step: *ikchapi* (one clap), *dochapi* (two claps), *sehchapi* (three claps) are typical variations to this dance.

Dhamal

Muslim fakirs (Holy men) perform *Dhamal* when they are in a wajd. In modern times the definition has changed to denote a Sufi trance dance, designed to attain union with the Divine. The sole goal of Sufis is to attain union with God. *Dhamal* is less constrained to rules and regulations of movement than the whirling dervishes of Turkey. It is a unique way to express a personal link with Divinity. No-one can dictate how an individual should experience the Divine in his life and the drumming to which *Dhamal* is done speaks directly to your spirit, by-passing dogma and inhibitions.

The whole experience of *Dhamal* is to lose control of yourself and to hand over your body to Divine energy.

Jhumar/Ghumar

The women of a family dance the *Jhumar* at weddings and the men lead marriage parties with the dance. Flat-footed striking of the ground and spasmodic clenching of the fingers is typical of this dance.

Khattak

A male performs this dance in a circle with swords and small scarves. Jerky movements are typical of this dance, accompanied by rapid twists of the wrists. Wide long dresses flow outwards during the dance.

Leva

The *leva* reflects the graceful movements of the camel and are mostly performed by men.

Luddi

This is the most popular dance at a wedding and expresses happiness and excitement. This is a group dance performed in

○ *Persian Sufi Dance, oil on canvas by Iranian artist Mohsen Keiany.*

a circle with clapping together towards the centre of the circle and snapping the fingers outwards.

Multani

This dance was also known as *Gate Ghore Ka Raqs*. The dancer slips into the body of a cardboard horse and performs the dance. Full size camels, elephants and horses are also added to the groups at times to create more excitement.

Zikr

Zikr is an ancient practice of remembrance from the Middle East. The word 'zikr' means remembrance and it is done with the intention of dropping the illusions which keep us trapped in ourselves, therefore opening up the freedom of self realization and is the inspiration of poets such as Rumi and Shabistari.

⬆ *An artist performing.*

⬆ *Sufi and Music by Iranian artist Mohsen Keiany.*

↑ *The Holy Dance by Iranian artist Mohsen Keiany.*

The basic form of *Zikr* uses the phrase La illaha illa llah. This phrase means, 'There is nothing but oneness.' It could also be translated as 'There is no Allah but Allah.' It is a very powerful statement because it takes us from our everyday concerns and places us in a universal cosmology.

In *Zikr* practice, while breathing out the first phrase, 'La illaha,' the head makes a sweeping motion from left to right and then straight up. You are saying, 'There is nothing.' This is a moment of cleaning out, of accepting the vast vacuum of space which permeates us, dropping your individual personality and personal concerns. This is a most important moment of the *Zikr* because, unless you clear out your heart's chamber there is no place for divinity to enter.

In the second part of the phrase, 'illa llah,' you breath in, filling up the lungs, first dropping the head down to the chest and speaking into the heart, and then raising the head to eye level. This is not a declaration as the first phrase, but more of an exclamation of wonder, 'accept oneness.' You have emptied yourself of everything and now divinity comes.

Zikr dances often incorporate other sufi phrases, movements and song. Long *Zikrs* can go for hours or days. Short *Zikr* practices are often done at the Dances of Universal Peace meetings.

Makhdoom Ahmad Chishti

References

1. Lights of Islam, Uxi Mufti, National Institute of Folk and Traditional Heritage, Islamabad(Pakistan), 2000.
2. www.mysticdance.com
3. www.starmeditation.com/dhamal

9

Cricket Versus Gulli Danda

Cricket is played all over the world. Even children play the game in streets and parks. As I was growing up I was surrounded by cricket fans – my father Mohammed Sarwar (may his soul rest in peace) and my brothers Mohammed Jahangir and Mohammed Fardos. When my brothers used to play with their friends, I would be sitting watching or sometimes even screaming for them to let me play. The comment I would receive back would be: 'You're a girl, girls don't play!' At that time they were right, but if we look at today's world, women play nearly all the sports, even cricket.

Throughout my childhood, cricket players were part of my experience, from Imran Khan and Javed Miadhad to Inzamam Ul Haq and Shohaib Akthar. But what inspired me to write this article is the film *Lagaan*, a super hit Bollywood film that starred Aamir Khan. In the film he tried to explain the game of cricket to the other villagers by using the term, *Gulli Danda*. This film made me wonder how far back did this game go.

There are several theories explaining how cricket started. It was said that shepherds in Southern England used to play. One would stand in front of a gate and another would throw a stone towards him, which he would have to hit with the bottom end of his crook.

The first ever cricket match is thought to have been in the 1300s, between Prince Edward and his friend Piers Gaveston. However, the first match ever recorded took place in Coxheath in Kent in 1646. Today's bat was invented around 1853. It developed from a shepherd's crook into a long, thin club, similar to a hockey stick straightened out. Then it became a blade made of willow with a cane handle layered with strips of

⊕ *Teams playing Gulli Danda in a multicultural sport festival at Birmingham Sports Centre, Balsall Heath, Birmingham in 1989.*

rubber tied in twine and then covered in rubber for a perfect grip. The early balls were stones, now they are made of cork and covered with a hand-stitched leather case that is dyed red.

The stumps are three posts but at one time there used to be two or four. The size also varied. In the seventeenth century the gap between them was up to two metres wide. The bails are the two bits of wood on top, and if they were knocked off during the game, then the whole game was over. Today, if the bails are knocked off, only the individual batsmen is 'out', not the whole team.

The game *Gulli Danda* is played by two teams, just like cricket. All that was needed was a stick and a widget or *gulli*, where both ends would be tapered. The stick would be no longer than one's forearm. It was not necessary to play the game on a grass field, as any open piece of ground would be acceptable. A furrow would be dug on this open ground into which the widget would be placed. As this was tapered at both ends, it was necessary for a player to strike one tapered end with the stick and the *gulli* would spin in the air and fly away from the furrow. The opposing fielder had to catch it so that the player would become 'out', but, if missed, then he would need to throw it towards the stick. If the *gulli* hit the stick the player would also be out. The object of this game was to count the number of lengths that the *gulli* was sent away and the team with the most lengths to its credit would be the winning team.

Gulli Danda is similar to cricket in that the player hits the ball as far out as possible, but as soon as the fielder catches it the striker/ batsmen is out. The similarity of cricket and *gulli danda* ends there unfortunately as in *Gulli Danda* there are no wickets, no wicket keeper and no ball. I suppose Aamir Khan was not that far off when he tried to explain the game!

Nayela Tabassum

10

Kabaddi

Over the past thirty years, *Kabaddi* has become a prominent and celebrated game amongst the Asian Communities in Britain. It is a 'crowd-puller' at the major Asian sports tournaments held every year across the country. *Kabaddi* has gained recognition and popularity and has become an established sport in Britain. Increasing television coverage since the mid 1980s has proved that *Kabaddi* can build an enthusiastic following as a spectator sport. In terms of participation, *Kabaddi* is an outdoor summer sport. However, during the winter season, indoor facilities are used for games and training purposes. In recognising the increasing popularity of *Kabaddi* in Britain, the Sports Council (UK) recognises *Kabaddi* as a British sports activity and included it as a Category 'C' sport in the prioritisation of governing bodies.

To Western eyes, the game looks like a mixture of tag and rugby, but minus the ball! Gradually, the game has evolved from a rural village game into a sport with specific rules governing all aspects of play and the size of the playing area. There are two distinct sets of rules, which apply to the two different playing courts, the rectangular and circular. *Kabaddi* has been likened to team tag, judo, and wrestling, but it includes a degree of tactical skill of its own. Requiring no special equipment (not even a ball), the game can be played on hastily improvised courts almost anywhere, using varying numbers of players. It is a uniquely accessible and fast game that is gaining a much more visible, and audible, profile far from its native home.

Kabaddi is a game, which originated in Asia but is especially popular in the Indo-Pakistan Sub-Continent. The game varies in different countries and is known by different names. In Pakistan, Bangladesh and India, it is known as '*Kabaddi*' or 'Kaudi', in Sri Lanka as 'Guddo', in Indonesia as 'Techile', in Nepal as 'Do-Do', and in Malaysia as 'Chaddo-Chaddo'.

There are two main styles of *Kabaddi*; a circular style and a rectangular style. The word '*Kabaddi*' means 'holding breath', which is a fundamental part of the version played on a rectangular court, and is favoured in Japan, Southern India and China. The circular version is more popular in Europe and Canada but it involves no holding of breath. Both seem popular in Britain, the circular game being on a larger pitch and being more physical, while the rectangular is a tighter and more tactical game. The game is played with virtually no equipment and is reliant on co-ordination of thoughts and action, strength, stamina, mobility and tactical skills. *Kabaddi* develops a strong physique, determination and a sense of responsibility.

The basis of *Kabaddi* lies in attaching and defending territory as well as overcoming the opponent. The players are called raiders and defenders. The beauty of the game is that players

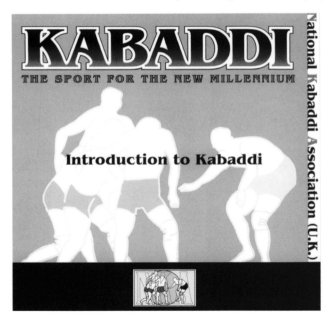

⬆ *Introduction to Kabaddi, produced by National Kabaddi Association (UK) in 1997.*

attack and defend at the same time. Physical strength and mental agility are the main qualities of a good *Kabaddi* player.

A good raider may play defensively, even though it means giving away points for unproductive raids, and the defenders will try to draw him deep into their territory while edging round in linked pairs or trios as he weakens with loss of breath. The entire process looks like a finely choreographed ballet. Or he may go swiftly into attack at the risk of being caught, using a low sweep of his outstretched leg, perhaps, to catch a defender unawares and then dashing back to his own side to confirm the kill. He may build up momentum for his raid, hopping from one foot to the other like a boxer, constantly on the move while perfectly balanced for a snap-action twist, turn, dodge, touch, and sprint home. He may grunt his chant and slap his thighs to intimidate his opponents, while never taking his eyes off their slightest movements. And even if trapped in a defensive circle, he will not give up as long as he has breath, for if he can just so much as graze with a finger or toe the centre line beyond which lies his home territory, every one of the defenders who has touched him will be deemed 'dead'. So he will try to leap the arms of a blocking chain, or duck under it, or simply barge his way back for a touch.

In rectangular styling the defenders act as an encircling seven-strong team throughout, and a raid lasts as long as the chant on one breath can be maintained.

The game may appear to be casual, but it is not quiet. A designated player from the team at one end of the court must venture into the other team's territory, touch as many opponents as possible, and return to his own court, all in one breath. To prove that he is not taking a breath, the raider continuously chants '*Kabaddi! Kabaddi! Kabaddi!*' The defenders must either avoid being touched, or block the raider and hold him in their own court until he loses his chant.

The Birmingham Pakistan Sports Forum has done much to popularise the game in Britain. It believes that an internationally regulated rectangular game will eventually become the standard. The National Kabaddi Association (UK), based in Birmingham has taken a leading role to develop awareness of the game at local and national level in the UK. Within this strategy, it is keen to see *Kabaddi* introduced into schools, and is positively working to develop versions of the game, which are suitable for women, children and girls, and people with disabilities. Birmingham is a home for *Kabaddi*. Each year, Small Heath and Cannon Hill Parks are home grounds for *Kabaddi*.

A new generation across different cultures will take to the rectangular version, because, in addition to needing strength and agility, the players must play a technical game. It is more tactical and greater fun. It can be played indoors, the court being about the same size as that used for badminton in schools. This was the version that the Commonwealth Games and the Olympics have encouraged.

Kabaddi was played as a demonstration sport at the 1936 Berlin Olympics. It is the National Kabaddi Association (UK)'s hope that, as one of the few games to win international popularity in a move from East to West rather that the other way around, it will be seen at the Olympics again before too long.

Makhdoom Ahmad Chishti

References

1. The Pakistan Kabaddi Federation, 'Rules of the game of Circle Kabaddi', Lahore, Pakistan, 1988.
2. Asian Amateur kabaddi Federation, 'Rules of Kabaddi', A.K. Saha, 2nd edition, 1988.
3. Yugesh Walia, 'Kabaddi', Channel 4 Television, Alpine Press, 1991.
4. Makhdoom A Chishti, 'Introduction to Kabaddi', National Kabaddi Association (UK), Connexion Design, 1997.

11

Persian Rugs

Mr Zareian, a businessman born in Iran, first came to the UK in February 1963. His first impressions were good and he thought that 'if heaven existed it would be here'. When he first arrived in the UK he went to evening classes to learn English, and within a few months he began to speak and understand the language. After approximately six to eight months he ran out of money and had to get a job in a factory, where he swept the floor. He worked hard and eventually his employer gave him a better job, which was filing papers. After eight months or so, Mr Zareian was given a job as a grinder. The money he earned was very good and he began to save. As time went by, within one year, he was able to put a deposit on a house, and after two years he bought a small café on Stoney Lane. After four years he left his work at the factory and became a self-employed businessman. Within seven years he had bought a shop in Selly Oak. Twenty years on, Mr Zareian still owns the shop in Selly Oak, which now sells Persian carpets. It is, he believes, the best rug shop in the West Midlands with the largest and most genuine selection of imported Persian rugs.

When Mr Zareian initially bought the shop in Selly Oak, it was a grocery shop, which he ran for about ten years, but when Sainsbury's came the shop was no longer viable. After much thought and consideration Mr Zareian decided to open a carpet shop to sell high quality, authentic Persian rugs. He was aware that since the Islamic Revolution in 1979, Iran's relationship with the West had deteriorated, but just as he opened his new store selling rugs, demand for genuine Persian rugs began to increase. The rugs sold in Mr Zareian's store are, he claims, approximately 30-40% cheaper than anywhere else in the UK.

It is very difficult to find two identical rugs. They are made either in the city by craftsmen or in rural areas by various tribes. Those created in the city are made by craftsmen sitting and

↑ *A rug from Shiraz made of a fine wool pile on a cotton base, showing a famous and very different traditional design.*

copying selected patterns. The patterns are commercially driven and the greatest emphasis is on colour and design. Those created by tribes are different. Each carpet tries to tell a different story. Those who create these rugs are passionate about how they create them and this helps to make them popular. Many traditions in carpet making have not changed for hundreds of years.

Those rugs made in the city have a 100% wool base and the tassels at the ends are made of cotton/silk. Tribal rugs are 100% woollen, they are hand twisted and are woven, and the tassels at the ends are made of wool. The colours are created by herbs and shrubs. All rugs are original; one would never find the same one twice. Prices range from £100 – £41,000 each depending on the quality, not the size of the rug. Carpets last for a very long time and are bought and sold. If they become worn they can be repaired by an expert craftsman who can convey the story which the rug is telling.

The quality of each rug is shown by its grade. Each rug possesses its own grade, which is measured by the size of the

⬆ *Mr Abdul Rasool Zareian (70) with the eldest of his six children, Deborah Reynolds (39), in his shop Oriental Rug Centre, Bristol Road, Selly Oak, Birmingham.*

knots which can be seen on the back of each rug. They are counted and then graded within a set measurement, for example 1cm. Grade one is the best and four is the lowest quality.

When he first came over forty years ago, Mr Zareian was young. He practised his religion but was not as sincere in his devotion as he is now. Since moving to the UK he has become stricter in his religious practice. Mr Zareian feels that if a person wants to practise his religion he needs the willpower to follow it correctly according to the guidance and teachings of Islam. He has found that over the years it has become increasingly difficult to practise Islam.

Mr Zareian feels that Muslims still have a lot to do world-wide in raising the awareness of Islam and what it teaches. It is very difficult to explain and practice Islam in non-Muslim countries as one is unable to express the sincerity of Islam to people. He feels that Muslims need to do a lot to explain the teachings of Islam and show the pure beauty and essence of Islam not just to Muslims but equally to non-Muslims. The aim should be to encourage Muslims, especially the younger generation, to pray and go to the mosque and learn about Islam.

Furkhandah J Sindhu & Aasma Nazir

12

The Minaret: a Symbol of Sacredness

Mosques are recognisable buildings in contemporary urban landscapes and minarets provide one of their most distinguishing features. In Birmingham, the minaret of the Central Mosque in Highgate has been a striking landmark for many years, but many people may not be fully aware of the origins and meaning of the minaret within Islamic culture. A simple definition is straightforward: a minaret is a slender tower attached to a mosque, surrounded by one or more balconies, which provides a means of calling Muslims to prayer. This article analyses the historical and religious background of the minaret as a symbolic icon in Islamic architecture.

Philologists were the first to investigate why a tower attached to a mosque should be called a Manar or Manarah, the Arabic words for minaret, which means the place of fire or a place of light. Some of them noted that the word might have been borrowed from the Aramaic word meaning candlestick or from the word Sawma'a, which is used in North Africa and Spain for a tower or a square minaret. In any case, the origins of the word are unclear.

Archaeologists and historians hold different opinions about the first appearances of the minaret as well. Oxford University's publications about Islamic architecture have traced the origins and varieties of the minaret to pre-Islamic towers in the Christian Syrian, late-antique Mediterranean world, ancient Mesopotamia, Sassanian (224-651 AD) Iran and India. The earliest minarets that have been discovered in Syria were square and consisted of several storeys. This became the normal type in North Africa and Spain. In Iraq a spiral form was popular, but this form of minaret is seen occasionally outside the country of its origin, as in the mosque of Ibn Tulun in Cairo, built between 876 and 879 AD. The Persians used lots of columns and other cylindrical forms in their pre-Islamic architecture. In the Islamic period, the Iranians favoured a cylindrical form – a tall column with an enormous capital – which is, in fact, the balcony for the muezzin to call for prayer. Needle-like or pencil shapes with one or more balconies present graceful profiles in Turkey. Minarets became decorative as well as functional elements within Islamic architecture.

Early Muslims felt the need for a unique way of summoning the faithful to prayer. The Jews used horns and the Christians a wooden clapper to bring people to worship. One explanation for the emergence of the minaret for this purpose is as follows. In the second years of hijrat (623-24 AD), Abdullah Ibn Zaid, one of the Prophet Muhammed's ✿ (PBUH) companions, had a dream that he heard a voice calling Muslims to prayer. Muhammed ✿ (PBUH) ordered his followers to mount the highest roof in the neighbourhood and

↑ *Mausoleum of Sultan Quotably in Cairo, 1472-1474.*

⊘ *Qutb minaret in the Quwwat al-Islam mosque, Delhi, India.*

⊙ *Minaret of Birmingham Central Mosque, Highgate, Birmingham.*

↑ *The great mosque of Al-Mutawwakil in Samarra, Iraq 848-852.*

⊘ *Selimiye Mosque in Edirne, Turkey, 1574.*

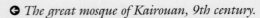
The great mosque of Kairouan, 9th century.
Friday mosque of Yazd, Iran, 1325 and later.
Minaret artefact, made in Egypt, contains verses from the Qur'ān.

call the faithful to prayer. Africans still use the roof of the mosque as a high platform for the call-to-prayer. Nevertheless, many historic mosques have no minaret. Scholars have argued that the minaret as a tower attached to a mosque appeared centuries after the beginning of Islam. Jonathan Bloom pointed out: 'Attaching a tower to a mosque and providing a distinctive place for the call to prayer were initially unrelated ideas that came together only centuries after the first mosque tower had been built. It was in the Abbasid (750-1258) period, not in the Umayyad (661-50) time as had already been thought.' (Bloom, 1989, p 175).

Later, when the Arabs defeated the Romans and conquered Damascus, they used part of St. John's Church as a mosque. They built four square towers or minarets as high platforms at the corners of the church to summon the faithful to prayers. Minarets became features of mosques from which the muezzin could give the call-to-prayer.

The number of minarets attached to individual mosques can mean different things. Repeating vertical forms as minarets, twice or more times, may signal the political or religious importance of a building. Different divisions of Islam have their own beliefs about the number and shape of minarets. For example, Shi'ite Muslims usually have two minarets in their mosques, whereas Sunni Muslims have one, five or four minarets, but there have always been exceptions. The single tower was accepted as a sign of the oneness of God in Islam. Then double minarets paired around a portal became a common architectural feature for composition purposes in architecture. The twin-tower feature arrangement remained standard for a long time in Iranian architecture in Timurid (1363/70-1502) and Safavid (1502-1736) architecture. One tradition derives from pre-Islamic times. Jonathan Bloom writes: the 'four towers standing guard at the corners of a roof had a long history in the architecture of the Near East. Four-towered temples were associated with the worship of a supreme sky god.' (Bloom, 1989, p.43)

The minaret represents the sacredness of the place of worship in the Islamic tradition. Throughout history, the minaret has always been a respected form in Islamic architecture that identifies a building as a mosque. As a result, it has become a symbol of Islam.

Mohsen Keiany

References

1. Bloom Jonathan, *Minaret: Symbol of Islam* (Oxford University Press, 1989).
2. Fiorani, Valeria Piacentini, 2003, *A Society without Cities* (BAR International series 1141, Milan, 2003).
3. Holod, Renata, *Architecture as Symbol and Self – identity*, Proceedings of Seminar Four in the series Architectural transformation in the Islamic Worlds (Morocco, 1979, viii). The Aga Khan award for architecture.
4. Hattstein, M and Delius, P (eds.), (2000), *Islam: Art and Architecture* (Konemann, Cologne, 2000).

Sources in Birmingham City Archives

Birmingham City Archives holds about 7,000 archive collections relating to Birmingham from the 12th century to the present day. Although recent work has uncovered information about the city's Muslim communities there is potentially much more information that could be unearthed with time and research. Potential sources include personal papers, the records of businesses, hospitals, schools, societies and organisations, and legal records such as court and coroner's inquest records.

The records of Birmingham City Council include a wealth of information about all aspects of life in the city including housing, health, education and transport. For example, the minutes of the Parks Committee for July 1942 discuss the establishment of a burial ground for 'Mohammedans' at Lodge Hill Cemetery in Selly Oak. The application was made by 'Mrs Mary

Amirullah, acting on behalf of the Moslem community resident in Birmingham', and the report mentions that at that time the only burial grounds for Muslims were in London or Cardiff. In 1956, when the Muslim community was estimated to be about

↑ *Headstone of Tunku Bahauddin's grave, son of Tunku Mahmood, died at Smethwick on July 30th 1942 and was buried at Lodge Hill cemetery, Selly Oak, Birmingham.*

↑ *Lodge Hill Cemetery, Selly Oak, Birmingham.*

↑ *Muslim graves in Lodge Hill Cemetery, dating from 1942.*

↑ *Rag Wali's grave, June 1945.*

↑ *Grave of Mariam Shah.*

↑ *Headstone of Mariam, daughter of Snoba Shah, buried in 1946, with engraved Shahadah.*

1,500 persons, the Pakistan Welfare Association applied for an extension to the burial area (BCC Committee minutes).

The records of other organisations in the city also often yield information. The Sparkbrook Association was formed in 1960 to improve social conditions and give advice to people living in the area. Dr Mollie Barrow was one of its main organisers and her papers and photographs refer to individuals and organisations such as the Pakistani Sports and Welfare Association who were active in the area (MS 1914). Funding applications by community groups such as the East African Muslim Welfare Association appear in the records of the Cadbury Trusts from the 1970s onwards and include information on the history of the group, their proposed project and ideas for the future (MS 1579).

Photographic archives can also be a valuable source for illustrating the lives of communities in the city. The archive of the 'Ten:8' magazine includes photographs by Nick Hedges of various religions in the West Midlands including scenes in mosques from the 1970s [MS 2478]. The photographer Tim Smith's collection includes photographs of Britain's South Asian communities, including those living in Birmingham (MS 2479), and Ghazala Saddique photographed the Lokmela festival in Birmingham, 1999-2000 (MS 2314).

Oral and video history is another rich source of information on people's experiences of settling and living in Birmingham. In 2000 the Millennibrum Project interviewed a number of the city's residents from a variety of different communities and backgrounds. Detailed interviews with people such as Dr Hanny El Banna, Zubair Khan, and Iffat Mir record their experiences and impressions.

⊙ *Dupatta (Asian scarf) stall at Lokmela 2000, Centenary Square, Birmingham. (Photographed by Ghazala Suddique)*

⊙ *Pakistani and Kashmir community at the launch of the Pakistan Youth Forum in 1984, in the Council Chamber, the Council House, Birmingham.*

⊙ *Delicious Lahori Kulfi at Lokmela 2000, Centenary Square, Birmingham. (Photographed by Ghazala Suddique)*

⬆ *Home and Away photographs of Britain's South Asian Communities by Tim Smith exhibition at Broad Street Gallery, Symphony Hall (27 October 2003 – 28 November 2003). The Lok Virsa Project was launched at the same time.*

Birmingham has longstanding economic, political and social connections with the wider world and many archive collections include information about other countries. Between 1889 and 1914 Helen Caddick travelled all over the world and kept a series of illustrated travel diaries recording her journeys. She visited Palestine, Greece, Egypt, China, Japan, India, North America, Java, Australia, New Zealand, South Africa, Mexico, West Indies, South America, Cambodia, Vietnam, Burma, Korea, U.S.S.R., Uganda, Kenya, and Ceylon (MS 908).

The Local Studies and History section of the Central Library holds newspapers, census returns, printed histories, oral and video history and photographic collections. The photographs collected and taken by the Birmingham photographer, Sir Benjamin Stone, document the people, architecture and landscape of the countries he visited including India, West Africa, South Africa and others.

Birmingham City Archives is keen to work with individuals and groups who are identifying and preserving historical records and recording the history of the city's various communities through oral and video histories, film, photographic and digital archives. For further information contact: Birmingham City Archives, Central Library, Chamberlain Square, Birmingham B3 3HQ; 0121 303 2468; archives@birmingham.gov.uk or see www.birmingham.gov.uk

Sian Roberts

14

The Collections at Birmingham Museums & Art Gallery

This article aims to introduce some of the collections held by Birmingham Museums and Art Gallery (BM&AG) that might be of particular relevance to those who are interested in the nature and influence of Muslim art and culture. Birmingham Museums and Art Gallery is the largest local authority museum service in England. The collections are of local, regional and national importance and encompass art, history, archaeology and anthropology. Drawing on the wealth of objects in the Museum's collection, BM&AG is planning to create an 'Islamic Trail' throughout the permanent displays, linking and highlighting items of particular relevance to Muslim visitors.

The art collections include painting, prints and drawings, sculpture, textiles and dress, ceramics, glass, jewellery, metalwork and furniture. Relevant objects and works of art tend to fall into three broad categories: work by Muslim artists, which is inspired or informed by Islamic heritage and tradition, objects originating from countries with Muslim cultures, and works by Western artists and designers working within visual traditions which take aspects of Islamic culture as sources of inspiration and influence.

In the first group, Anwar Shemza's paintings and prints combine the forms of Arabic calligraphy with Western abstract art. Shemza trained in Lahore and settled in Stafford in 1962, where he lived until his death in 1985. 'Meem' is one of a series of works based on the initial letter of the name of the Prophet Muhammad 🕌 (PBUH). In 'The Wall' the linear, flowing and repeating patterns are partly inspired by the carved marble screens found in Mughal architecture.

The second group comprises a wide range of material, some acquired in the earliest years of the Museum's history. From Iran, the major traditions of ceramics and metalwork are represented by small but striking groups of objects, dating from the 15th to the 18th centuries. A bottle vase is covered with trailing floral designs; a turquoise dish depicting a seated prince is beautifully painted in coloured enamels and gold. Tile panels, including some from Turkey and Syria, show how Islamic designs were part of an architectural environment. Several pairs of iron shields and helmets, skillfully inlaid with gold, show how calligraphy became an integral part of other art forms. The Southall Collection is an outstanding collection of Palestinian dress dating from about 1900 to 1930. These garments show the dyeing, weaving and embroidery techniques in use during this period. They also show some of the different styles of men's and women's dress worn in the towns, villages and by the nomadic Bedouin people.

The third category reflects the interests of many British artists and designers, several of whom travelled to North Africa and the Middle East or studied Islamic art in museum collections in London during the 19th century. Their work is significant in its representation of Muslim cultures and people, particularly women. W J Muller travelled to Greece and Egypt in 1838-1839 and the Museum has several works relating to his experiences there, including 'A Street Scene in Cairo' and 'Prayers in the Desert', which was painted using models after his return. J F Lewis lived in Cairo for ten years from 1842. His rich, detailed paintings, produced for a Victorian market, clearly originate from a Western Orientalist perspective. 'The Harem' and 'Lilium Auratum' both portray an 'exotic' femininity, strongly associating women with flowers and lavish textiles.

William De Morgan had a strong interest in Middle Eastern art and he studied ceramics and textiles in the South Kensington museum in the 1870s. BM&AG have a major collection of De Morgan pottery, which shows how the designer drew his inspiration directly from Islamic techniques, shapes, styles and motifs. It includes bowls, plates, vases and tiles and is of two main types. Firstly, De Morgan developed what he named 'Persian' colours – greens, blues and purples on a white background, in imitation of

↑ 'Street Scene in Cairo' by W J Muller, 1839 (18885P2530)
© Birmingham Museums & Art Gallery.
↺ 'The Wall', Anwar Shemza, 1958-1985 (1998P81).
© Mary Shemza.

⬆ *Palestinian dress dating from about 1900 to 1930, Southall Collection [Source: Birmingham Museums & Art Gallery].*

pottery made in Iznik (actually in Turkey). Secondly, he created a range of stunning metallic glazes, attempting to revive and reproduce the complex lustre technique, which originated in Egypt in the 8th century, spreading to Iraq, Iran and from there to Spain and Italy. The designs combine animals, flowers and foliage, clearly inspired by traditional Islamic motifs and patterns.

Historical examples of Islamic art were also an important influence on the work of William Morris, particularly the dense, flat floral patterns of Persian carpets. The Museum holds a group of his original designs and samples of many printed and woven textiles produced by Morris & Co., as well as part of his personal reference collection, which includes embroideries from Iran and Turkey.

F & C Osler was a Birmingham-based firm which opened an office and showroom in Calcutta in the 19th century. It specialised in cut glass and produced chandeliers, lamps and ornaments for export to British communities in India. Technical innovations enabled its trade to expand to include large pieces of furniture such as chairs, tables and even staircases and fountains. Much of this cut glass furniture was made to order for Indian palaces. A glass prayer mat in the collection is thought to have come from the great mosque in Bhopal. Made from six panels of thick cut glass, with mirror glass beneath, the distinctive *mihrab* arch-shaped design would have caught the light and reflected it into the building.

Zelina Garland

↑ *Plate, Iran, 12-13th century (1890M163).© Birmingham Museums & Art Gallery.*

15

An Islamic and Middle Eastern Heritage Collection in Birmingham

Birmingham's people and its institutions have played a vital role in getting the Mingana Collection to the city. Even so, it must be one of many heritage collections about which very little is known in Birmingham where it has been housed for over seventy five years. The collection consists of heritage items coming to us through centuries of human intellectual and artistic development. They represent the intellectual activity of many centuries in the fields of religion, philosophy, literature, philology, science, and art and design. Each manuscript represents the richness of language and expression, scientific knowledge, the skills of paper and parchment maker, the scholar, the scribe, the pen and ink maker, the illustrator, and the binder.

These materials were collected early last century between 1925 and 1929 from Middle Eastern countries through the endeavours of Dr Edward Cadbury, the Chairman of Council of Woodbrooke College (a Quaker Studies centre) and a founding member of the Selly Oak Colleges, as well as being one of the city's prominent businessmen. He sponsored and endowed the Collection, housing it in the Selly Oak Colleges Library, and naming it after its collector, Alphonse Mingana. The Collection has since moved to purpose-build modern premises, and is now part of the vast range of Special Collections of the University of Birmingham.

The Collection consists of mainly Arabic and Syriac Middle Eastern manuscripts. There are in addition, papyri and documents, a few Genizah fragments from Cairo, and examples of Armenian, Coptic, Ethiopic, Greek, Hebrew, Persian and Turkish manuscripts. There are also numerous works in Garshuni (Arabic in Syriac characters), a few coins, seals and a few clay tablets. The Collection has a four-volume printed catalogue. A recent publication is a catalogue of the Collection's illustrated manuscripts compiled by Prof. Lucy-Anne Hunt.

The Arabic manuscripts are the third largest collection in the UK. The Islamic Arabic manuscripts, c. 2000, are mostly religious. There are several copies of the Qur'ân, two collections of fragments of Kufic Qur'âns dating from the eighth and ninth centuries AD. Other works include Qur'ân commentaries, Hadith, law, literature, science and mysticism. Microfiche copies exist and are widely distributed to researchers and libraries throughout the world. They are also cited in Brockelmann's *Geschichte der Arabischen Literatur* (1930s), a reference work known to scholars worldwide.

↩ *Examples from the Mingana Collections, University of Birmingham. (Arabic Islamic 4/2000).*

Alphonse Mingana, the collector of the manuscripts, was born in the region of Mosul in Iraq in about 1878. He was educated at the Syro-Chaldean seminary in Mosul, and ordained priest in the Chaldean Church. From 1902-1910 he was Professor of Syriac at Mosul. His wide scholarly output included many editions of hitherto unknown Syriac and Arabic texts. In 1913, on the invitation of J. Rendel Harris (the first Principal of Woodbrooke), Mingana came to England, and spent two years at Woodbrooke College, Selly Oak. In 1915 he was appointed Curator of Oriental Manuscripts at the John Rylands Library, Manchester, where he stayed until 1932. During these years he came to know Dr. Edward Cadbury, at whose expense he travelled to the Middle East to purchase manuscripts. In 1924 and 1925 he travelled through regions of Iraq, Syria and Palestine, and in 1929 went to Sinai and Upper Egypt. Many of the manuscripts were bought from monasteries and private libraries in these regions. He returned to Selly Oak, and until his death in 1937 undertook the project of cataloguing the Collection. Though his interest was mainly in Eastern Christianity, his knowledge of Islam enabled him to lecture on Islamic history and literature as well. This work continued after his death by establishing a Lectureship in Islamic Studies, which evolved into the Centre for the Study of Islam and Christian-Muslim Relations in 1976, and which is now part of the School of Historical Studies in the University of Birmingham.

Meline Nielsen

◉ *Book with flap and decoration on the inside cover, al-Kalimat al-ʾaliyya al-ʿAlaviyya, Sayings of ʿAli ibn Abi Talib (died 40 AH/661 AD) Arabic in Naskhi script with Persian verses in Nastaʿliq script 976 AH/1568 AD.*
[Source: Mingana Collection, University of Birmingham, (Arabic Islamic 522/1651)].

⬆ *Small Qur'ân – miniature copy in reddish leather case, Iran, 12th/18th century.*

⬇ *Prayer scroll – Arabic (Naskhi), Woven silk scroll. Iran, 16th century. [Source: Mingana Collection, University of Birmingham, (Arabic Islamic 1650)].*

⬇ *Masnavi-i ma`navi by Jalal al-Din al-Rumi (died 672/1273) Persian, vocalized Naskhi script with explanations in Nasta`liq script in margins, Iran, 19th century. [Source: Mingana Collection, University of Birmingham, (Persian 1)].*

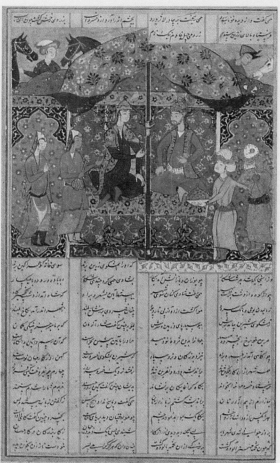

Qur'ânic chapters: Surat al-Fatiha, Ayat al-Kursi, of Surat al-Baqara. Arabic and Persian, Naskhi and Nasta`liq scripts (Iran) 1224 AH/1809 AD. [Source: Mingana Collection, University of Birmingham, (Arabic Islamic 1305/1636)].

The marriage of Khusraw Parwiz and Shirin – reproduced from the Mingana Collection of Oriental manuscripts held at the Central Library of the Selly Oak Colleges, Birmingham.

al-Kafi fi `ilm al-fara'id `Uthman al-Hifzi ibn Mustafa al-Dimatuqawi (died 1222/1807), Arabic and Ottoman Turkish, Naskhi script 1255/1839. [Source: Mingana Collection, University of Birmingham, (Arabic Islamic 1989/152].

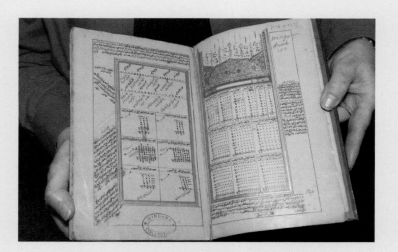

Glossary

AD Indicating years numbered for the supposed year of the birth of Christ.

AH Indicating years in the Muslim system of dating, numbered from the Hegira (622 AD) (the departure of the Prophet Muhammad ∰ (PBUH) from Mecca to Madinah).

Abdullah praised (prayer).

Adhan The call to Salah.

Akhirarh Life after death.

Allah The name for God in the Islamic religion. The one, supreme and only God, the Creator of the world and all humankind.

Al-amin meaning 'Trustworthy' which was one of the titles of the Prophet Muhammad ∰ (PBUH).

Al-Faruq The title of Khalifah 'Umar meaning 'the distinguisher between right and wrong.'

Aqabahis A place just outside of Makkah where the Muslims from Madinah pledged allegiance to the Prophet Muhammad ∰ (PBUH).

Arkanul Islam The five pillars of Islam.

Arabic The language and writing of the Arabs.

Asadullah Lion of Allah. One of the titles of Khalifah 'Ali.

Aws A tribe in Madinah.

Ayah Literally translates as a 'miracle' or 'sign'. This is the smallest unit of the revelation contained in the Holy Qur'ân.

Badr The place, 128km south-west of Madinah, where the Muslims fought the first battle against the infidels of Makkah.

Baitullah The house of Allah in Makkah.

Balti The Balti is an Indian dish representative of a style of cooking which some say is native to Baltistan. It's a kind of curry.

Bengali Bengali is an Indo-Aryan language and evolved from Sanskrit. The vast majority of the people of Bangladesh speak Bengali (Bangla).

Bhangra Bhangra is a lively form of music and dance that originated in the Punjab region in South-East Asia.

BM&AG Birmingham Museums and Art Galleries.

Chishti The Chishti order of the Sufis derives its name from Chisht (pronounce: Chesht, hence Cheshti). Chisht is a small town near Herat in Afghanistan. The first one to call himself Chishti was Abu Ishaq Shami. As the name Shami implies he came from Syria or even from Damascus (ash-Sham). He met a Sufi who directed him to settle in Chisht and from that day on he is known as Abu Ishaq Shami Chishti.

CE The Christian Era and used instead of AD in Islamic text, referring to the dates before the Hijrah.

CPD Continuing Professional Development.

Darul Uloom An Islamic madrassa or seminary.

Dhamal Dhamal is a Sanskrit word that originally referred to fire-running by Muslim fakirs (Holy men). In modern times that definition has changed to denote a Sufi trance dance, designed to attain union with the Divine.

Dhikr Refers to both memory and speech. When the Qur'ân is translated into English, passages that refer to 'remembering Allah' could be translated as 'invoking Allah'.

Dhul Hijjah the twelfth month of the Islamic calendar, when Hajj is performed every year.

Dholak A folk musical instrument.

Din Meaning way of life, religion.

Eid Islamic Festival.

Eid Al-Adha Feast of sacrifice. It concludes the Hajj and is a three day festival recalling Ibrāhīm's willingness to sacrifice his son in obedience to Allah.

Fatwa A ruling given by a person well versed in the Qur'ân.

Farsi The Persian language is the most widely spoken member of the Iranian branch of the Indo-Iranian languages, a subfamily of the Indo-European languages. It is the language of Iran (formerly Persia) and is also widely spoken in Afghanistan and, in an archaic form, in Tajikistan and the Pamir Mountain region.

Fiqha Literally 'understanding'. The term refers to the science of Islamic law or jurisprudence.

Eid Al-Fitr A three day Islamic feast marking the close of Ramadan. A festival of thanks giving to Allah for the enjoyment of the month, it involves praying and the fostering of understanding other religions.

Ghamkol Sharif A Sufi saint.

Ghusal The act of washing the whole body for Taharah.

Gulli Danda An Asian sport.

Hadith Recorded teachings of the Prophet Muhammad ﷺ (PBUH) outside of the Qur'ân.

Hafiz A person who memorises the whole Qur'ân.

Hajj Mandatory pilgrimage to Makkah during a predefined period. Each Muslim who has the means is required to perform this trip at least once in his or her lifetime.

Halal Lawful.

Haraam Unlawful.

Henna A herb which produce red colour.

Hidayah Guidance from Allah.

Hijab A Muslim woman's veil or head-covering when meeting strangers and going out.

Hijrah/Hijri The migration of the Prophet Muhammad ﷺ (PBUH) from Makkah to Madinah.

Hira' The cave in Mount Nur where the first revelation of the Qur'ân was revealed to the Prophet Muhammad ﷺ (PBUH) by the Angel Jibra'il (Gabriel).

Ibadah Meaning 'worship'. This is any activity performed to gain Allah's pleasure.

Iblis The devil or Satan who disobeyed Allah and swore to lead humans away from the word of Allah.

Ihram The special attire worn during Hajj.

Iman Meaning 'faith' or 'belief'.

Imam One who leads the prayer.

Injil Title used for the book known by Christians as the 'New Testament' and considered by the Qur'ân to be divinely revealed.

Iqra Translated as 'read', which was the first word of the Qur'ân revealed to the Prophet Muhammad ﷺ (PBUH) at cave Hira'.

Islam This is the name given by Allah to the religion for mankind. The word means submission and obedience to Allah's commands.

Jahannam Hell, the place of eternal suffering.

Jama'ah The name given to when people congregate and say Salah in a group.

Jamiah Central.

Jat The name given to tribe among Rajputs; an agriculturist.

Janazah The funeral Salah.

Jannah Heaven, the place of eternal bliss.

Jhumar A Punjabi dance.

Jibra'il The angel (Gabriel) who brought Muhammad ﷺ (PBUH) revelation from Allah.

Jinn Allah's creatures with free will, created from smokeless fire.

Jizyah The tax that is levied on non-Muslims of an Islamic state.

Jumadal Akhirah The sixth month of the Islamic calendar.

Káaba The first place built for the worship of Allah, in Makkah.

Kabaddi An Asian sport.

Kameez Asian female's top dress.

Khalilullah Friend of Allah. The title of the Prophet Ibrāhīm.

Khazraj A tribe of Madinah during the Prophet Muhammad's ﷺ (PBUH) time.

Khan A surname used by Pathans.

Keyammat Day of Judgement.

Khutbah The sermon given before Salatul Jumu'ah.

Kiraman Katibun The angels who write down everything that a human does on Earth.

Kutubullah The books revealed by Allah.

Labaas Dress.

Lagaan Agricultural tax.

Lok An Urdu word, meaning world, region or people.

Luddi A folk dance in the Indian sub-continent.

Madinatun Nabiyy The city of the Prophet Muhammad ﷺ (PBUH), commonly shortened to Madinah.

Madrassa A school where Islam is taught.

Maghrib Name of the Salah (prayer), just after the sunset.

Makkah The city where the Káaba is located and the birth place of Prophet Muhammad ﷺ (PBUH).

Malakul Mawt The Angel of Death (also known as Izra'il).

Mahr A dowry; the money or its value incumbent on the husband.

Masjid An Arabic word meaning mosque.

Mirpur A city, situated in Azad Kashmir.

Mirpuri People from Mirpur.

Mohsen A benefactor, an individual person's name.

Millah Nation or community.

Millatun Wahidah One nation.

Mi'raj The ascent of the Prophet Muhammad ﷺ (PBUH) to Heaven.

Mufti A person who is qualified to give a Fatwa on Islamic ruling.

Mujahid Warrior.

Mujahidin Warriors.

Mulana A person respected for learning.

Mumin Believer of Islam.

Muhammad ﷺ (PBUH) The final messenger of Allah to mankind. His name was Muhammad bin (son of) Abdullah.

Namaaz Prayer.

Nasheeds Religious songs.

Nikah Meaning marriage between a man and a woman.

Nisab A Muslim's annual savings on which payment of Zakkah is compulsory.

Nur/Noor Allah's light. Angels created from Nur.

PBUH These letters are abbreviated for the words 'Peace Be Upon Him.' They are widely used by English speaking Muslims for all the prophets.

Punjabi Person from the Punjab.

Pushto Language largely spoken in the north of Pakistan.

Qada Making up for a missed prayer.

Qiblah The direction to the Káaba in Makkah. Muslims face the Káaba during formal prayer.

Qur'ân The infallible Holy Book. It contains the word of Allah in its original form without any modifications.

RA Radiallahu Anha (may Allah be pleased with her).

RH Radiallahu Anhu (may Allah be pleased with him).

Rabi'ul Awwal The third month of the Islamic calendar.

Rasul A messenger from Allah.

Riba Interest payments, which are unlawful in Islam.

Ruh The name for the soul that lives on after death. It also refers to the angel Jibra'il in the Qur'ân.

Ruku' Bowing during Salah.

Safar Second month of the Islamic Calendar.

Salah/Salat The compulsory prayer, offered at five set times everyday.

Swam Fasting in the month of Ramadan, one of the pillars of Islam.

Shában Eighth month of the Islamic calendar.

Shahadah Testifying that 'there is no God but Allah, Muhammad ﷺ (PBUH) is Allah's messenger.'

Shaheed A Muslim who sacrifices their life for the sake of Allah.

Shaitan The Arabic word for devils or evil forces from Jinn.

Shalwaar Trousers, mostly worn with Indian sub-continent dress.

Shari'ah Way, path, law or code of conduct.

Sheer-Khurma A sweet dish (made with milk and vermicelli), usually made on Eid-Al-Fitr.

Sheikh A venerable old man; a chief of a tribe or of a village.

Shiá A follower of Caliph Hazaret Ali (RH).

Shirk Meaning associating partners with Allah which is the most severe of sins and will not be forgiven.

Sufi An abstemious person; wise.

Sunnah 'Way' or 'custom', 'the way of the prophet Muhammad 🕌 (PBUH)', commonly known as the Prophet's traditions.

Sunni Orthodox Muslims.

Swaiyaan Vermicelli.

Sylhet A city and region situated in Bangladesh.

Tafsir Detailed explanation of the meaning of Qur'ân.

Tabriz A city, situated in Iran.

Tahajjud Optional Salah, between midnight and dawn.

Taqwa Abstinence; one who fears Allah.

Torah The book revealed to Prophet Musa (Moses) (PBUH) by Allah.

Ummah Arabic word, meaning the Muslim Nation.

Umrah The shorter pilgrimage to the Káaba in Makkah at any time of the year.

Urdu A language of the Indian Sub-continent, meaning an army of languages composed mainly of Arabic and Persian words.

Virsa An Arabic word meaning heritage.

Wajib Obligatory.

Wudu Washing/cleansing for Salah in a prescribed way.

Yawmuddin The Day of Reckoning or of Judgement, in the life after death.

Yawmul Akhir The last Day or the Day of Judgement.

Zakah A compulsory welfare contribution payment from a Muslim's annual savings.

Zuhr The obligatory prayer to be offered at noon.

Notes on Contributors

Dr Tahir Abbas is a member of Birmingham's Pakistani community and Senior Reader in the Department of Sociology and Director of the Centre for the Study of Ethnicity and Culture at the University of Birmingham. He has written widely on the Muslim experience in Britain and contributed to newspapers, television and radio programmes.

Dr Gëzim Alpion was born in Albania and is a Lecturer in Sociology at the University of Birmingham. As well as publications on the media and cultural themes, he has written plays and published articles in the national, international and local press.

Makhdoom Ahmad Chishti was born in Pakistan and came to the UK in 1976. He is chairperson of the Social Unity Foundation of Innovation (SUFI) Trust Ltd and created the Lok Virsa Project. He is Senior Equality and Diversity Officer in Birmingham City Council and is involved in the work of several statutory and non-statutory organisations. He has written many articles on sport, Asian culture, music and Muslim life. his latest publication was 'Introduction to Kabaddi'. His voluntary work is an inheritance from his great-grandfather's social work after 1886 and his inspiration comes from his father's saying: 'live for others'.

Verdah Chishti is a Youth Development Officer for the Youth Offending Service, Social Care and Health in Birmingham. Verdah holds a degree in Law and Sociology and is involved with numerous community projects in a voluntary and non-voluntary capacity. Verdah is currently studying for a master's degree in Clinical Criminology and aims to develop her career in community welfare work.

Dr Malcolm Dick has worked on several community history projects and was Editor and Director of the Millennibrum Project from 2000-2001. He currently lectures in the Centre for Lifelong Learning and School of Education at the University of Birmingham. Malcolm has published material on the history of education, refugees, migration and the history of Birmingham. His latest book is *Birmingham: a history of the city and its people* (2005).

Professor Saeed Durrani is a scientist by training and an author. His writings are inspired by Allamah Dr Sir Mohammed Iqbal, the poet-philosopher of the East. Currently, he is chairperson of the Iqbal Academy (UK) and has been serving as a leading member of many organisation and institutes. Professor Durrani worked formerly in the Physics Department at the University of Birmingham.

Zelina Garland is Curator for Applied Art in the Interpretation and Exhibitions Team at Birmingham Museums & Art Gallery.

Alison Gove-Humphries is an adviser in the CPD/Equalities team at the School Effectiveness Division, Birmingham. She has taught history for thirty years, co-ordinated Black History Month in schools and co-published a teaching pack entitled 'We Also Served' on African, Caribbean and Asian veterans in the World Wars.

Mohsen Keiany was born in Iran and lectured in Art at the University of Shiraz before he came to live in Birmingham. He is a teacher and artist and has exhibited widely in Britain and abroad. Mohsen is currently studying for a PhD on Muslim architecture at the University of Central England.

Jahan Mahmood was born in Birmingham and has Pakistani and Afghan ancestry. He graduated from the Centre for Lifelong Learning at the University of Birmingham in 2003 and completed a special study of Birmingham's Afghan population. He is employed in Birmingham as a community worker and as a visiting lecturer at the Centre for Lifelong Learning.

Izzy Mohammed is the Community Access Officer for the Connecting Histories project. He graduated from the University of Leicester and began a career in the museums sector. His experiences reinforced the view that a chasm lies between mainstream cultural provision and where marginalised communities are found. His current work through Connecting Histories is an attempt to redress imbalances and to democratise opportunity.

Aasma Nazir graduated from university in Pakistan and is undertaking a master's degree in Management in Public Services at the University of Birmingham. Previously she managed a national pilot road safety scheme in Birmingham and now is working as External Funding Co-ordinator in the Sparkbrook District where she supports local community and voluntary groups to develop projects and secure funding. Through involvement with statutory and non-statutory organisations, she has gained knowledge and experience of community development work.

Meline Nielsen was the Librarian of the Selly Oak Colleges, and the Manager of the Orchard Learning Resources Centre, prior to joining the Special Collections department of the University of Birmingham Information Services, where she is currently the Collections Care Manager. She is also the keeper of the Mingana Collection of Middle Eastern manuscripts, and joint Curator of the 'Illuminating Faith: Art and Culture from the Middle East' exhibition at Birmingham Museum & Art Gallery, supported by the Heritage Lottery Fund.

Siân Roberts has been Head of Archives for Birmingham City Council in Birmingham Central Library since 1997. From 2005 until 2007 she is on secondment as Project Manager for the Connecting Histories Project, funded by the Heritage Lottery Fund. Siân was also co-convener of the Black Pasts, Birmingham Futures Group and in 2002 edited *Making Connections: Birmingham Black International History* with Ian Grosvenor and Rita McLean.

Furkhandah Jabien Sindhu is married with one child. She graduated from Aston University in 2004 where she obtained a degree in Human Psychology and Biology and hopes to begin Primary PGCE training at the University of Birmingham. She has been a volunteer for several years with various organisations including the Acorn's Children's Hospice, student volunteers, the National Mentor Pilot Project Scheme and the SUFI Trust.

Nayela Tabassum is married with one child. She is a housewife. In her spare time she works for charity organisations as a volunteer, she has been inspired to take up a course in leadership and management. Her hobbies are reading, watching television and listening to music.

Adam Yosef is a British journalist who specialises in community, socio-political and current affairs. He writes for the Midlands newspaper *The Asian Today* and is a weekly columnist for the national entertainment tabloid *Desi Xpress*. He also contributes to the BBC and is a former employee of the Birmingham Mosque Trust.

SUFI Trust Appeal First Aid & Ambulance Centre in Khanewal, Pakistan

Imagine that one of your family members or colleagues needs urgent medical attention. You would call for an ambulance, which would arrive in a few minutes, and take them to the A&E Department at your local hospital.

Imagine what would happen if there were no ambulance or emergency facilities, and if the main hospital was 50–100 miles away. This is the situation in Khanewal, a small town in the south of Pakistan with a population of over 250,000 people.

The SUFI Trust has initiated a project to set up an Ambulance Service and build an Emergency Centre to provide emergency care in Khanewal but this cannot be achieved without your support.

To achieve our aim we are looking for your help and assistance. We need to raise £2.5 million to build the Emergency Centre and run the Ambulance Service.

The cost per casualty is about £10 and you could consider supporting 10 casualties per year. Your £10 will save not only one life but will help a whole family, consisting of 7 to 8 people.

The SUFI Trust has co-ordinated relief aid to the affected areas of Pakistan and Kashmir, in partnership with St. John Ambulance (UK) and Birmingham Central Mosque following the devastating South Asia earthquake disaster in 2005, and sent 20,000 blankets as well as medical aid.

The ambulances bought by your donations will be working in areas where people do not have any access to immediate medical treatment, shelter, food and clean water.

Please make cheques payable to "SUFI TRUST". Or you can deposit your donations directly into a bank. Our accounts details are as follows:

Bank: HSBC
Account Number: 71649752
Sort Code: 40-11-15
International Bank Account Number (IBAN): GB20MIDL40111571649752
SWIFT Code: MIDLGB22

Postal Address:
SOCIAL UNITY FOUNDATION OF INNOVATION (SUFI) TRUST LTD
7 Rolling Mill Close
Edgbaston
Birmingham
B5 7QD

● *Volunteers packing goods donated at Birmingham Central Mosque for the Pakistan and Kashmir earthquake in 2005.*

◐ *Handing over the ambulance keys ceremony (these ambulances were donated by the West Midlands St. John Ambulance for use in Pakistan): Lord Mayor Councillor Mike Nangle (patron: SUFI Trust), Anwer Al-Nisa (patron: Baha Jee Social and Welfare Association, Khanewal, Pakistan) and Susan Taylor (County commander, St. John Ambulance, West Midlands County) [Courtesy: Evening Mail, August 28, 2004].*